Jesus Keeps Showing Up

Philip Gladden

Parson's Book Publishing
Porch. & Company

Jesus Keeps Showing Up
ISBN: Softcover 978-1-946478-22-1
Copyright © 2017 by Philip Gladden

All rights reserved. No part of this book may be reproduced or transmitted in any form or by any means, electronic or mechanical, including photocopying, recording, or by any information storage and retrieval system, without permission in writing from the publisher.

Cover art by Luc Freymanc. www.freymanc.com.

To order additional copies of this book, contact:

Parson's Porch Books
1-423-475-7308
www.parsonsporch.com

Parson's Porch Books is an imprint of **Parson's Porch & Book Publishers** in Cleveland, Tennessee, which has double focus. We focus on the needs of creative writers who need a professional publisher to get their work to market, **&** we also focus on the needs of others by sharing our profits with those who struggle in poverty to meet their basic needs of food, clothing, shelter and safety.

Jesus Keeps Showing Up

Dedicated to the faithful members of the Wallace Presbyterian Church, Wallace, North Carolina, with gratitude to God.

Philippians 1:3-11

Table Contents

In That Great Gettin' Up Morning 11
    1 Kings 17:1-24; Acts 9:36-43

Preaching and Propriety 17
    Luke 4:16-30; Amos 7:7-17

Too Much at Ease 23
    Amos 6:1-7; Luke 16:19-31

A King and A Cross 30
    Luke 23:32-43; Colossians 1:11-20

A Church Full of Zebras and Ostriches 36
    Galatians 5:13-15; Romans 1:1-17

When Words Fail Us 42
    Romans 8:18-30

God from A – Z 47
    Titus 2:11-14; Psalm 111

Home 53
    Hebrews 10:19-25; Psalm 84

Spiritual and Religious 59
    Mark 12:28-34; James 1:17-27

Thank You, Jesus! 65
    Jeremiah 31:31-34; Hebrews 10:11-18

Don't You Worry 'Bout A Thing 70
    Matthew 6:25-34; Philippians 4:4-7

Famous Last Words 77
    Numbers 6:22-27; 2 Corinthians 13:11-13

What Does God Want from Me? 84
    Romans 12:1-2; Micah 6:1-8

It's Go Time! 91
    Ephesians 1:2-14; Matthew 28:16-20

A Cruciform Church 96
    Colossians 1:15-20; Hebrews 12:1-2

Jesus Keeps Showing Up 102
    John 20:1-18; John 20:19-31

The Dance of Love 108
    Isaiah 6:1-8; Romans 8:12-17

Sacred Cows and Best Practices 114
    Exodus 20:1-17; Mark 7:1-23

My Whole Life Long 120
    Romans 8:31-39; Psalm 71:1-24

God's Future for The Here and Now 127
    Galatians 3:23-29; Revelation 7:1-17

The Goal of Love 132
    Leviticus 19:11-18; Romans 12:14-21; Matthew 5:43-48

Home for Christmas 139
    Matthew 11:2-6; Isaiah 35:1-10

Putting Joseph in the Manger Scene 145
    Isaiah 7:10-17; Matthew 1:18-25

In Line with Sinners 151
    Romans 6:1-11; Luke 3:1-22

The Jesus Paradox 158
    Colossians 1:15-20; Mark 9:9-13, 30-37

May I Have This Dance? 164
    Romans 12:1-2, 9-21; Mark 10:32-45

In That Great Gettin' Up Morning
1 Kings 17:1-24; Acts 9:36-43

When my wife and I served as co-pastors of the Littleton Presbyterian Church in Halifax County, NC, we often worked with the Blaylock Funeral Home, which was located just around the corner from the church. As we got to know the men who worked at the funeral home, one of them in particular began to share some funeral stories with us.

One story was about Sister Pauline's funeral. Her funeral was held in a little church out in the country. The sanctuary was packed and seven or eight preachers spoke in turn. The funeral home man said that each preacher seemed to be trying to outdo the previous preachers. As a result, the service started running to two hours, then three hours. For a long time, he stood patiently by the back door of the sanctuary, because he wanted to display a professional and respectful image. However, he finally got tired of standing up, so he sat down on the back pew.

Sister Pauline was laid out in an open casket in front of and just below the pulpit. The funeral home man said that one of the last preachers began to lean over the pulpit and preach directly to Sister Pauline in her casket. "Sister Pauline, in the name of Jesus Christ, I command you to get up!" He repeated the message several times, getting louder and more animated each time he said it. The funeral home man ended his story by saying, "I decided I didn't care how unprofessional it looked — if Sister Pauline got up, *I* was going to get up and get out the front door as fast as I could!"

Maybe that's why Luke tells us that "Peter put all of them outside" the upper room before he said, "Tabitha, get up." In the eight short verses of this story from Acts 9, we hear about the stark confrontation between the cruel reality of death that can take away a beloved disciple who was devoted to good works and acts of charity, and the victorious power of the resurrection in the name of our risen Savior Jesus Christ.

This story about Peter and Tabitha and the Christian community at Joppa begs the question: Why doesn't God still raise people from the dead through the words and presence of his ministers and believers? Some Christians claim to have this power from God, while others are very skeptical of those very claims of the dead being raised in the 21st century.

As I thought about this story from Acts, I tried to frame it in the very personal terms of my pastoral care as the minister of this congregation. I can relate to Acts 9:38, when two men come to Peter with the request, "Please come to us without delay." The phone rings, I answer it, and someone says, "We need you at the hospital right away" or "Can you come to the house as soon as possible?" Let's be honest here: I've never responded to any call like that with the intention of going into the hospital room or the home and commanding someone to "Get up!" from the dead. Also, I don't think I've ever been called by a family that had the expectation that I would do what Peter did in that upper room in Joppa, no matter how much they might want it to happen for them and their loved one.

Why is that? Is it because we don't have enough faith? Is it because we don't really believe in the power of God to raise the dead, despite our glorious Easter worship service in here just three weeks ago? If I did go into a hospital room or a home, pray to God over a church member who had died, tell the member to "Get up!" and he or she didn't get up, what would that say — about me as a minister? about the gospel promise of the resurrection? about my faith in God's power to bring life out of death? about our church?

While we can certainly ask those questions after reading about Peter and Tabitha in the upper room, I'm not sure they are the most appropriate questions for us to think about. Maybe the better question to ask is, "Where is God's resurrection power at work in other ways, in our lives, in our church, in our community, and in our world?" Maybe that's the better question, because the power of death doesn't just show itself when someone's heart quits beating. The powers of sin and death are just as much at work when we shut ourselves off from what God is stirring up with the fresh breezes of the Holy Spirit. The powers of sin and death are just as strong when we are afraid to live as bold disciples of Jesus Christ, and instead are content to go along with the status quo. The powers of sin and death are certainly a challenge to this community of faith when one of our beloved members dies. But sin and death are also a challenge when the church doesn't live out of God's strength and power which have been shown so forcefully in the resurrection of Jesus Christ from the dead.

At the conclusion of his notes about this story from Acts 9, Professor James Boyce of the Luther Seminary in St. Paul, Minnesota writes, *"This story will not answer all our questions. For example, why do we not today experience the same resurrection of loved ones that was given to Tabitha and the early Christian community? But what the story does bring is the clear and certain witness to the power of our Lord's resurrection, and to the good news that not only at times of death, but at other dark times, the Spirit of the risen Lord enters our world to bring life and healing and hope."*[1]

Listen again to Professor Boyce's last phrase: *"The Spirit of the risen Lord enters our world to bring life and healing and hope."* Three weeks ago we came here to worship and celebrate the good news of Jesus Christ's resurrection from the dead. Inevitably on Easter Sunday, talk of the resurrection makes us think about life everlasting, life after death, eternal life, life beyond the grave. There is certainly nothing wrong with that hope and celebration on Easter Sunday. In fact, today's sermon title is taken from the famous spiritual by Mahalia Jackson called "In That Great Gettin' Up Morning." Looking to the future, the song says,

> *Let me tell ya bout the comin' of judgement*
> *Fare thee well, Fare thee well*
> *God going up and speak to Gabriel,*
> *Pick up your silver trumpet.*
> *Blow your trumpet Gabriel.*
> *Lord, how loud shall I blow it?*
> *Oh, to wake the children sleepin'.*
> *They be comin' from every nation*
> *Dressed in a white robe, so white as snow,*
> *Singin', Oh, I've been redeemed.*
> *In that great gettin' up morning.*
> *Good news, good news,*
> *So glad chariot's comin',*

*And I don't wanna be left out
In that great gettin' up morning.
Fare thee well, Fare thee well.*

But the resurrection of Jesus Christ — and the power it packs — is also for you and me, for the church, right here and now. When Jesus' friend, Lazarus, died, Jesus consoled his sister, Martha. Jesus said to her, "Your brother will rise again." Martha said to him, "I know that he will rise again in the resurrection on the last day." Jesus said to her, "I am the resurrection and the life. Those who believe in me, even though they die, will live, and everyone who lives and believes in me will never die. Do you believe this?"

"Do you believe this?" On this fourth Sunday of Easter, after the handbells have been packed away, and the brass and timpani are no longer playing so majestically in this sanctuary, now that the Easter lilies have given way to spring flower arrangements at the front of the church, do we believe this? Do we believe that Jesus is the resurrection and the life? Not just some day in the future. Not just some day when we die. But right now, in the midst of death and darkness and life's challenges. Do we trust in God's power to bring life out of death when our own Tabithas die and leave big holes in the fabric of our congregation's life and ministry?

Why all this talk about resurrection? The Bible has stories about other people being brought back to life, not just Tabitha. We have to assume they eventually died again. But the power behind their new lives was the same power that raised Jesus from the dead on Easter, the same power the Creator of the whole universe used, the same power that is available to Christ's church to fulfill our calling as his disciples and the people of God.

In the midst of "success" stories in the church in Acts 9 & 10, we come upon two stories where the "success" is threatened by the darker realities of life and death. Earlier in chapter 9, we read, "Meanwhile the church throughout Judea, Galilee, and Samaria had peace and was built up. Living in the fear of the Lord and in the comfort of the Holy Spirit, it increased in numbers." (Acts 9:31) Just after the story of Tabitha and Peter we read the story about the conversion of Cornelius and his household, Gentiles who believed the gospel and were filled with the Holy Spirit.

In the midst of these "success" stories, we read about Aeneas, who had been bedridden for eight years, for he was paralyzed (9:32-35) and Tabitha, a disciple devoted to good works and acts of charity, who became ill and died (9:36-43). Not even saints and believers full of good works and acts of charity are immune to physical limitations and death. Our community of faith has to deal with our own loss and grief when a beloved Tabitha passes away. But, as these stories tell us and as we celebrated three weeks ago, death will not have the final say.

Peter told Aeneas, "Jesus Christ heals you; get up and make your bed!" Peter told Tabitha, "Get up." The word for "get up" is the same word for "resurrection." We need to listen to what Luke is saying in these nitty-gritty stories in the midst of church growth, success stories: There is a power loose in our world and in our lives, a power that can change our ways of death into ways of life — that power is the resurrection of Jesus Christ.

In his commentary on the book of Acts, William Willimon says of these stories about Aeneas and Tabitha, *"Every time a couple of little stories like these are faithfully told by the church, the social system of paralysis and death is rendered null and void. The church comes out and speaks the evangelical and prophetic 'Rise!' and nothing is ever quite the same."*[2]

Perhaps you and I and the elders are not called, in this time and place, to raise people from the dead. Perhaps God's power is at work in different ways in our lives and in this church. But there is no doubt that we are called to trust in God's life-giving power in the face of apparent dead-ends and in opposition to the status quo that cuts us off from the new things God has in mind for us and our church. Instead of fretting about why we can't say to a dead person, "Get up!" maybe we can listen for the Lord telling us to "Get up!" When we Christians are paralyzed by fear and ravaged by death, we can be more trusting of the One who has the power to "help us up," as Peter helped up Tabitha in the upper room.

At the risk of repeating myself, I'd like to share with you part of what I wrote in my April newsletter article (from Sam Miller's book, *The Life of the Soul*). It seems so very appropriate to this story about Peter and Tabitha and its message to us in the church today: "*We fear failure more than we love life, so we refuse the great ventures. We are careful to do only what we have always done and know how to do well, so we never break the dull repetition of the old routine for the new creation in God. Crawl out of these tombs and prisons — there is a world of light and freedom waiting! Have faith in God and let life be free. Stop riding the brakes on the heart. The soul will never grow, tied down in bed, with the shades drawn. The higher and more secure we build the barricades of care and caution to protect ourselves, the deeper grows the grave we call our life.*"[3]

If we sincerely trust in the power of God to raise Jesus Christ from the dead, and to make that same resurrection power available to us in the church today, then every morning can be "that great gettin' up morning!"

NOTES

[1] James Boyce, "The Success of the Apostolic Mission: Acts 9:36-43," *Preaching This Week*, Lectionary for April 25, 2010, at www.workingpreacher.org.

[2] William H. Willimon, *Acts* (Atlanta: John Knox Press, 1988), p. 86.

[3] Samuel Miller, *The Life of the Soul* (Waco, Texas: Word Books, 1951). Shared with me by Rev. Larry Williams on the March 2010 retreat at the Avila Retreat Center near Durham, NC.

Preaching and Propriety
Luke 4:16-30; Amos 7:7-17

"Once upon a time, there was a quiet little village in the French countryside, whose people believed in Tranquilité — Tranquility. If you lived in this village, you understood what was expected of you. You knew your place in the scheme of things. And if you happened to forget, someone would help remind you. In this village, if you saw something you weren't supposed to see, you learned to look the other way. If perchance your hopes had been disappointed, you learned never to ask for more. So through good times and bad, famine and feast, the villagers held fast to their traditions. Until, one winter day, a sly wind blew in from the North . . ."

As the narrator speaks those words over scenes of the French villagers gathering for worship at the local church, the movie *Chocolat* begins. In the tranquil setting of that little church, when the sly North wind blows the church doors open, everyone is startled. The mayor, Comte de Reynaud, who tends to all of the details of the church, is obviously irritated when the doors blow open. He stalks down the center aisle and, as he slams the doors shut against the wind, the narrator emphatically repeats, "Tranquility!"

The mayor's mission is to maintain order in the town and in the church, just as his ancestors did. The new village priest, Pere Henri, is a wide-eyed, wet-behind-the-ears minister who has a weakness for Elvis Presley's music. He has only been in town five weeks. His predecessor had served for fifty years. Comte de Reynaud pays the priest regular visits. In one scene, the mayor tells Pere Henri he has finished looking over his Sunday sermon, and has made "just a few suggestions." As he hands the sermon to the priest, you can see the many deletions and corrections and suggestions in the margins.

As the movie develops, the mayor is determined to get rid of the newly arrived stranger and her daughter, who have opened a chocolate shop during the season of Lent. Again, Comte de Reynaud pays a visit to the priest, tells him "You have to know who your enemies are," and asks him what he is going to do about this woman. The next Sunday, the priest nervously preaches a condemning sermon, specifically naming the chocolate shop as one of Satan's tools. As the camera pans to the mayor sitting on the first pew, you see his lips moving, perfectly synchronized as he mouths the words of the priest's sermon. On Easter Eve, Pere Henri and the Comte de Reynaud are in the mayor's office, "reviewing" his Easter sermon. The mayor is relentless in his coaching and his suggestions to the priest — "It has to be perfect tomorrow, to inspire the members of the congregation!"

I won't give away the ending of the movie, but suffice it to say, after some interesting developments overnight with the mayor and the chocolate shop, Pere Henri finds his own voice in the pulpit on Easter Sunday morning. As he looks out on his congregation, many of whom have had their lives transformed by the woman in the chocolate shop, Pere Henri lays down his manuscript of his sermon and says, *"I'm not sure what the theme of my homily today ought to be. Do I want to speak of the miracle of Our Lord's divine transformation? Not really, no. I don't want to talk about His divinity. I'd rather talk about His humanity. I mean, you know, how He lived His life, here on Earth. His 'kindness,' His 'tolerance' . . . Listen, here's what I think. I think that we can't go around . . . measuring our goodness by what we don't do. By what we deny ourselves, what we resist, and who we exclude. I think . . . we've got to measure goodness by what we 'embrace,' what we create . . . and who we include."*

Let me be quick to say, Mayor Charley Farrior (an elder in the Wallace Presbyterian Church) has never once edited one of my sermons, nor has he called me to his office down the street to "practice" my sermon with me! Having made that perfectly clear, I have to say I could sympathize with Pere Henri in the pulpit. It has been said that the task of the preacher is to "comfort the afflicted and afflict the comfortable." You might sometimes say, "He's gone from preachin' to meddlin'" or "He stepped on our toes today." Or, you might not sometimes not say anything at all. When that happens, I usually have a lot to think about on a Sunday afternoon.

If the movie *Chocolat* had been set in 8th century B.C. Israel, Amaziah, the priest of Bethel, would have had the role of Comte de Reynaud. Amos, the prophet of God, might have played Pere Henri, who found his voice in the pulpit, despite what Amaziah thought about his message. Amaziah misrepresented Amos' message to King Jeroboam II. Then he tried to run Amos out of town — "flee away to the land of Judah, earn your bread there, and prophesy there; but never again prophesy at Bethel, for it is the king's sanctuary, and it is a temple of the kingdom." If Amaziah had had a bumper sticker protesting Amos' message, it might have said, "We don't care how you did it down south in Judah!"

In his official capacity as the royal priest — the head of staff of the biggest church in town — Amaziah worked hard to maintain "tranquility." When a new wind blew into Bethel in the person of Amos of Tekoa, Amaziah did his best to keep the temple doors closed against the Word of the Lord. His report to King Jeroboam sums up his own attitude toward and actions against the prophet Amos: "The land is not able to bear all his words."

Where is the line between preaching and propriety? Should there even be such a dividing line? In a way, I'm preaching to myself this morning, and you're invited to listen in. Many of the constraints I feel in the pulpit are actually self-imposed: What will people think? Should I say that? How will that be received? Should I even go there? Is this God's Word to his people or just my opinion?

At the end of our second year in seminary, we had to take what were called "evaluative reviews." They were three weeks of exams on just about anything and everything in the seminary curriculum. You had to pass to continue your seminary education. Talk about a lot of stress and pressure! One exam was to write an exegesis paper about a psalm and produce a sermon based on your work. I think the psalm might have been #46, which says in verse 3, "Do not put your trust in princes, in mortals, in whom there is no help. When their breath departs, they return to the earth; on that very day their plans perish."

Ronald Reagan had just been inaugurated as president four months earlier. He came into office with great expectations among the American people at large, and with great promises. Well, I thought this new presidency was an appropriate and timely illustration for my sermon on Psalm #146, so I used it. I didn't think I was making an overtly political statement. I was just trying to write a sermon and pass an exam. After all, I had only written one or two other sermons in my life at that time. When I got my sermon back, the professor had written across the top something like, "This is nothing but a liberal Democratic diatribe!" [Obviously I passed anyway, or else I wouldn't be preaching here this morning!]

One Sunday I preached at First Presbyterian Church in Rocky Mount, North Carolina when my wife and I were on staff there. I preached a sermon in opposition to the death penalty. After worship, a church member came up to me and said, "Do you know who was visiting in church today? Judge So-and-So! He's presided over lots of capital punishment trials, and he probably didn't agree with what you just preached." To this day I still wonder if the person was saying, "You shouldn't have preached that in this church" or if the person was simply commenting on the judge's presence.

In a commentary on the scene at the temple of Bethel, when Amaziah confronted Amos about his preaching, one writer says, "The criterion for what could be said at Bethel was quite clear: that which was proper, fitting, suitable for such a place as the royal chapel. Propriety, in other words, determined the content of the preaching allowed there."[1] That is a deadly trap for a preacher — tailoring your message to what's "acceptable" or, as the prophet Micah says, *"Thus says the Lord concerning the prophets who lead my people astray, who cry 'Peace' when they have something to eat, but declare war against those who put nothing into their mouths."* In other words, it's tempting to shape sermons according to one's salary.[2]

We can be so at ease sometimes, so complacent, so "tranquil" that we ignore the needs and injustices and opportunities that are all around us. Even worse, we can so want to be at ease and tranquil, we will shut the doors of the church to any and all winds of change from God that might blow among us and through our church. As I told the Wednesday morning Bible study group this week, working on this sermon was a humbling experience for me. Who am I in the story? Am I more like Amaziah, the priest of Bethel, who was on the temple payroll? True confession: I cringe when someone refers to me as a "church professional." I don't want to be a "church professional." I just want to do what God has called me to do, a big part of which is proclaiming God's Word to God's people (me included!). Or am I more like Amos? Just to ask that question sounds so self-serving and, in some ways, pompous. But Amos told Amaziah, "Look, I'm not a professional prophet, and it's not my family business. The Lord took me from what I was doing, and the Lord said to me, 'Go, prophesy to my people.'"

One of the greatest gifts a church member has ever given me was something Juanita Powell told me one day after Bible study. I must have seemed nervous about what I was going to preach on Sunday. Juanita came up to me, looked me in the eye, and said, "You go ahead and preach what you think God is telling you to say. We can take it."

Preaching from the Word of God is a wonderful, awesome, and terrifying privilege and opportunity. Sometimes I get to preach the comforting words of scripture. Sometimes I'm convicted to preach the more challenging Word of the Lord. Either way, I try to listen for God's Word in my heart before the first word ever comes from my lips. As you get ready for weekly worship, I ask you and encourage you to spend some time with God's Word for that weekly sermon. Ask God to open your hearts and lives to the wind of God's Holy Spirit that can blow through, around, under, and over our efforts always to keep things "tranquil."

In 1979, Bishop Fulton J. Sheen was the speaker at the National Prayer Breakfast in Washington, D.C. President Jimmy Carter and First Lady Rosalynn Carter were sitting in the first row of the audience. Bishop Sheen began his remarks by addressing the audience as "my fellow sinners." Then he turned to President and Mrs. Carter and said he was including them as well. Some people were offended at the impropriety of the bishop's remarks. But, in his own remarks, President Carter said, "it even boosts my spirits when he refers to me as 'fellow sinner.'"

Friends, that's who we are, you and I — "fellow sinners" who need to hear the Word of the Lord in its fullness. Thanks be to God for his living Word. May we always have humble hearts to preach and hear God's Word.

NOTES

[1]James Limburg, *Hosea-Micah* (Atlanta: John Knox Press, 1988), p. 119.

[2]Ibid.

Too Much at Ease
Amos 6:1-7; Luke 16:19-31

I am the 48,489,298th richest person in the world.

I'm in the top .8% of the world's population in income.

If we consider our annual church budget to be the equivalent of a family's annual income, our church would be the 107,565th richest family in the world, in the top .001% of world income.

At least, that's what www.globalrichlist.com indicates. This is an interesting website posted by a group called "Poke" out of London. They base their calculations on figures from the World Bank Development Research Group. To calculate the most accurate position for each individual [they] assume that the world's total population is 6 billion and the average worldwide annual income is $5,000.[1] The people who have posted the "Global Rich List" make the interesting observation that most people gauge their personal wealth by comparing themselves to people who have *more* than they do. They say when we do that, we think of ourselves as poorer than we really are. The folks at "Poke" are trying to provide a different perspective and — as they are upfront in claiming on their website — trying to raise money for good causes.

The "Global Rich List" has its critics who say it doesn't take into account vast differences in the cost of living around the world and the calculations are too broad to be of much use to anyone. Proponents of the website are more forgiving, and point out that it's a helpful tool to put our level of income in some kind of global perspective. If you want to be more exact, visit some of the available websites that have data about global per capita income. You can crunch some numbers and discover (no great surprise) that if you live in the United States, you're better off than the overwhelming majority of the world's citizens.

Another way of coming at this is to think about the world as a village of 100 people. Perhaps you've seen this breakdown. The figures I'll give you seem to be typical of many different versions of this hypothetical situation.

"If the world were a village of 100 people, with all existing human ratios remaining the same, the demographics would look something like this:

> * The village would have 60 Asians, 14 Africans, 12 Europeans, 8 Latin Americans, 5 from the USA and Canada, and 1 from the South Pacific.
>
> * 51 would be male, 49 would be female.
>
> * 82 would be non-white, 18 white.
>
> * 67 would be non-Christian; 33 would be Christian.
>
> * 80 would live in substandard housing.
>
> * 67 would be unable to read.
>
> * 50 would be malnourished and 1 dying of starvation.
>
> * 33 would be without access to a safe water supply.
>
> * 39 would lack access to improved sanitation.
>
> * 24 would not have any electricity (and of the 76 that do have electricity, most would only use it for light at night).
>
> * 7 people would have access to the Internet.
>
> * 1 would have a college education.
>
> * 1 would have HIV.
>
> * 2 would be near birth; 1 near death.
>
> * 5 would control 32% of the entire world's wealth; all 5 would be US citizens.
>
> * 33 would receiving — and attempting to live on — only 3% of the income of the "village."[2]

Are you uncomfortable yet? I am, so let me say upfront, I'm preaching to myself just as much as I'm preaching to anybody else here this morning. Jesus' parable about the rich man and Lazarus is another of Jesus' hard sayings, coming on the heels of the difficult parable from last week about the dishonest and shrewd manager. Last week's gospel lesson was difficult because it was hard to figure out why Jesus would tell a parable about a dishonest man who was commended for what he had done with his master's accounting books. Today's parable is difficult, not because it's hard to understand, but because the message is challenging. As Mark Twain famously said, "It ain't those parts of the Bible that I can't understand that bother me, it is the parts that I do understand."

Coupled with the Old Testament reading from Amos 6, Jesus' parable really packs a punch. Amos was a southerner from Judah, who preached to the folks up north in Israel during a time of peace and prosperity. As the introduction to the book of Amos in my study Bible puts it, "Amos was called by God from a shepherd's task to the difficult mission of preaching harsh words in a smooth season." It should come as no surprise that Amos wasn't very popular up north. In fact, the king's court prophet, a guy named Amaziah, told Amos to go home: "Flee away to the land of Judah, earn your bread there, and prophesy there; but never again prophesy at Bethel, for it is the king's sanctuary, and it is a temple of the kingdom." (Amos 7:12-13)

Again, the study notes in my Bible describe Amos' message in chapter 6 as being directed at "the Israelites, who feel themselves secure in their false confidence and lie upon beds of ivory in luxurious self-indulgence." If the old adage is true about a preacher's job being "to comfort the afflicted and afflict the comfortable," Amos was a pro. A couple of biblical commentators were pretty blunt in their assessment of Amos' message. One said, "A little of Amos goes a long way." Another one said, after skillfully laying out the truth of Amos' message and its application to our lives as God's people, "I don't think I like Amos much." I'd like to think that both comments were made tongue-in-cheek, but we're probably all saying "Amen!" under our breath right about now.

I'm not in the pulpit today to harangue the rich which, if we put any stock in "The Global Rich List" or "If the World Were a Village of 100 People" or any of the numerous studies about global income and wealth, would include every single one of us in this sanctuary, relative to the rest of the world's population. In the same way, Jesus doesn't appear to judge the rich man because he was ***rich***. In fact, one of the main and surprising twists of this parable is the great reversal of fortunes for the rich man and Lazarus.

The Pharisees who heard this parable would have been surprised, because it was a commonly accepted and pretty well supported-by-the-Old-Testament idea that riches were a blessing from God. Also, there is no indication that the rich man in the parable did anything dishonest, illegal, or unethical to become rich. And yet — ***and yet!*** — the rich man comes under judgment. What's going on here?

The rich man's downfall was not his riches, but what he allowed his riches to do to him. For whatever reason, he let his riches come to preoccupy him, so much so that he ignored the needs of a poor, sick man named Lazarus who had, literally, been dumped on his front-door step. The real indictment of the rich man in the story is, his wealth prevents him from seeing or relating to Lazarus as a fellow child of God. It's not reading too much into Jesus' parable to say that the man's riches on the one hand, and his neglect of Lazarus on his doorstep on the other, suggest that he thought he was self-sufficient in life. The rich man sounds a lot like the rich farmer who looked at his harvest and his barns and said to himself, "I'll tear down these barns and build bigger ones; then I'll be set for life." That night he died — and, in the same way, in today's parable, "the rich man also died and was buried."

This parable is called "The rich man and Lazarus." One blogger has suggested that the parable could be called "The-Indifferent-Man-Who-Could-Have-Listened-to-Moses-and-the-Prophets-and-Followed-God's-Way-of-Life-and-Been-Welcomed-Into-Paradise-by-Father-Abraham-But-Chose-Not-To and Lazarus." When the rich man begged Father Abraham to send Lazarus back to warn his brothers to change their ways, Abraham said, "They already have what they need to know about doing God's will. If they do not listen to Moses and the prophets, neither will they be convinced even if someone rises from the dead." We need to hear Father Abraham's words in light of the fact that Luke wrote his gospel some fifty years after Jesus died and was raised again from the dead. In other words, we have Moses and the prophets (think Amos!) AND someone who has been raised from the dead telling us what it means to live in community with the people around us.

Jesus is quoted as saying, "You always have the poor with you, but you do not always have me" when Mary anointed his feet with expensive perfume and Judas objected at the extravagance of the act. We could hear Jesus saying, in a resigned tone of voice, "You'll always have the poor with you, and there's nothing you can do about it." That would let us off the hook pretty easily. Or, we can hear Jesus saying, "Her act is one of pure love at a time of my need, but you'll always have the poor with you. There will always be plenty of opportunities for you to respond. Her spontaneous love for me does not neglect the poor."

In fact, our love for the Lord can lead us — **should lead us** — to care for those very poor as fellow children of God. I came across an interesting blog this week by a Baptist minister in Clinton, Mississippi, which he called "Blogging Toward Sunday: Great Chasm." Listen to his experience as he reflects on this parable from Luke:

"I spent most of the day after Hurricane Katrina checking on members, especially older ones, in and around Clinton, Mississippi, where I live. Clinton did not sustain serious damage, but we lost all power and lots of trees and roofs, and there was a palpable sense of fear and anxiety. Cars lined up immediately for gas, stores closed, evacuees packed the shelters, and the locals feared a serious shortage or crisis.

"At the end of a long, hot and unnerving day, I was heading home to a cold shower when I received a call from my friend David in Nashville. He had one question: "Have you checked on the poor?" The thought hadn't occurred to me, so I turned my car around and drove back toward the hidden neighborhood where the poor mostly reside in our town.

"In our town it's possible to go a long time without seeing the poor. A beautiful parkway lined with flags and flowers enables us to drive across town without driving through the neighborhoods leading to the poor. We do a pretty good job of keeping them hidden. My friend David must have been watching television coverage that we residents had not yet seen. On my trip back into town, I found a family I knew that had recently been evicted and were living in an uncle's shack. They were without any provisions, and all the stores were closed, so I went to a

family in our church. They cleaned out a cupboard of peanut butter, bread and bottled water. This was a brave gift, since they did not know when power and provisions would return.

"It is ironic and tragic that I had to be reminded to remember the poor; I'm a pastor, after all. I have spent years studying the scriptures, and I like to think I know them pretty well. So, why did I forget the poor in a time of crisis?

"The rich man thought he knew scripture too. He thought they were his stories; he possessed the stories enough to think himself a child of 'Father Abraham,' as he said. But he turns out tragically to have overlooked the heart and soul of scripture — the story of God's deep desire to create a people of hospitality and welcome for the poor and the stranger."[3]

In October 2000, we held a homecoming here at the Wallace Presbyterian Church as part of our year-long celebration of the new millennium. One of our former ministers, Rev. Jim Atwood, was our preacher that day. He stood right here where I am standing and said to us, "I'm afraid the church is at ease in Zion." I think Jim is right, and I wrestle with what to do about it, as a person of faith and as a minister.

As the buckets were passed this morning for our "Feed Our Hungry Children" offering, you could hear the coins hitting the bottom of the pails. Isn't that how it feels sometimes? Like what we do is nothing but a drop in the bucket? I don't know about you, but this parable from Luke 16 and Amos' message have pricked my conscience. God has certainly richly blessed us, as individuals and as a church. God has raised Jesus from the dead, and he has told us and shown us how to live as God's children. The question is, will we listen even to someone who has been raised from the dead?

We have these words printed on our United States currency: "In God We Trust." As someone has said, "If we do actually trust God, then we will take to heart God's injunction to have compassion on those around us, to be vulnerable to each other, to actually see God in the face of our neighbor's need."

NOTES

[1] See "Global Rich List" at www.globalrichlist.com.

[2] See "If the World Were a Village of 100 People" at www.familycare.org/special-interest/if-the-world-were-a-village-of-100-people

[3] Stan Wilson, "Blogging Toward Sunday: Great Chasm," at www.theolog.org/2007/09/bloggin-toward-sunday-great-chasm.html

A King and A Cross
Luke 23:32-43; Colossians 1:11-20

Here is a series of events from this past week, seemingly random, but upon further reflection, perhaps not random at all:

One day after work, I stopped by Wal-Mart on the way home to pick up some things for supper. I took my place in the "20 items or less" line and settled in to wait. When I glanced up, I saw the back of a T-shirt on the guy a couple of people ahead of me. The T-shirt had a picture of a 6 point buck and these words: "It's Good to Be King."

This week I came across the words to Bruce Springsteen's song "Badlands," in which he sings, "Poor man wanna be rich/Rich man wanna be king/And a king ain't satisfied/Till he rules everything."

The media are agog over the news of the engagement and pending marriage of Prince William and Kate Middleton. A spring or summer 2011 wedding is expected, perhaps at Westminster Abbey. There are already reports that some royal watchers in Britain are urging the media to refer to the bride-to-be as "Katherine" instead of Kate. Also, there is some head-shaking and tongue-clucking because, after all, "Katherine" is a commoner. Then there are the connections with Prince William's mother, Princess Di, whose ring William gave to his fiancée.

As I was driving down I-40 the other day, I listened to a story on WHQR about the new movie, "The King's Speech," about the unexpected ascension to the throne of Albert (known as King George VI) after the abdication of his brother, Edward, who married Wallis Simpson. Albert never expected to be king. Further complicating matters, he was reluctant to speak in public because of a severe stammer.

The director of the movie also directed the mini-series "John Adams," based on David McCullough's book. There is a dramatic scene in "John Adams" when John Adams, newly appointed representative of the recently liberated United States of America to the defeated British, is ushered in to meet King George III. There is much tension and build-up as Adams approaches the room where King George is waiting. The rooms are huge and palatial. Adams looks appropriately awed. Then the door to the meeting-room is opened.

There stands King George beside the throne, resplendent in his red coat and sash. However, he and the others in the room are dwarfed by the size and splendor of the room. When the director of the movie was asked about his staging of this scene, he said he wanted to convey the impression that King George III could never live up to the mythology and expectations surrounding the British monarchy.

John Adams is portrayed as reluctantly bowing to King George as he enters and leaves the reception room. It is obvious this newly appointed representative of the independent United States of America is not comfortable with the royal protocol. His uncomfortable body language is very symbolic of what's going on between him and the King. Just as Adams is about to leave the room, King George calls out to him, "Mr. Adams!" Then the king says, "Mr. Adams, I pray that the United States of America will not suffer for wont of a monarchy." John Adams looks at the king and says, "Your majesty, we will work hard to fulfill your prayers."

And finally, today is Christ the King Sunday on the church calendar, the final Lord's Day in the church year. Next Sunday we begin the season of Advent, which also marks the beginning of the church year and leads us to the celebration of the newborn King. Christ the King Sunday also marks the end of what is called "Ordinary Time" on the church calendar, a misleading misnomer if there ever was one. Ordinary Time runs from the day of Pentecost through Christ the King Sunday. The name suggests that nothing special happens in the life of the church for six months. But that's hardly the case. Actually, Ordinary Time is the time when we hear about the life and ministry of Jesus and reflect on what it means to be his faithful disciples.

So, perhaps the events of this week weren't so random after all.

- It's good to be king.

- And a king ain't satisfied/Till he rules everything.

- Kate Middleton is the first commoner to marry into the royal family in 350 years.

- King George VI works hard to overcome his stammer so as to represent the British monarchy more appropriately.

- The pomp, circumstance, and majesty of King George III's reception room make John Adams nervous and he is very apprehensive about meeting the king.

There is an obvious concern about the dignity and power and majesty and presentation of "the king" in all of these varied examples. Then we come to the scripture reading from Luke's gospel for this Christ the King Sunday: "they crucified Jesus there with the criminals . . . The soldiers also mocked him, coming up and offering him sour wine, and saying, 'If you are the King of the Jews, save yourself!' There was also an inscription over him, 'This is the King of the Jews.'" (Luke 23:33, 36-38)

Where is the pomp? Where is the circumstance? Where is the protocol? Where is the majesty? Where is the power? What we have instead is a dying man hanging on a cross, being chastised and mocked by the Jewish religious leaders and the Romans soldiers. The irony of this story, of course, and the challenge for all of us who cherish our independence, is that the inscription on the cross is 100% true. Look at the man on the cross. Not only is he the "King of the Jews," he is the King of kings, the Lord of lords, and he shall reign forever and ever.

When Queen Elizabeth II took the throne in 1952, her private secretary asked her what her royal name would be. She answered, "Why, my own! What else would it be?" Actually, her official royal designation began with "Her Majesty Elizabeth the Second, by the Grace of God, of Great Britain, Ireland and the British Dominions beyond the Seas Queen," and included twenty-seven different regal names, including Sovereign of the Most Honourable Order of the Garter, Sovereign of the Most Excellent Order of the British Empire, Sovereign of the Most Exalted Order of the Star of India, Sovereign of the Royal Order of Victoria and Albert, and Sovereign of the Most Venerable Order of the Hospital of St John of Jerusalem.

Compare those titles with what Colossians says about our King on a cross: "He is the image of the invisible God, the firstborn of all creation, for in him all things in heaven and on earth were created, things visible and invisible, whether thrones or dominions or rulers or powers – all things have been created through him and for him. He himself is before all things, and in him all things hold together. He is the head of the body, the church; he is the beginning, the firstborn from the dead, so that he might come to have the first place in everything."

On Sunday, November 21, 2010, in the midst of national and global and, perhaps, personal economic turmoil, what does King Jesus have to do with us? In the face of airport security screenings and pat-downs, what does King Jesus have to do with everyday life? In the day-in, day-out, nitty-gritty realities of getting through life, what meaning do those lofty, majestic titles of King Jesus have?

Well, I left out the last description of King Jesus in Colossians 1:19-20, in which all of the other titles come together with the greatest significance for your life and mine: "For in him the fullness of God was pleased to dwell, and through him God was pleased to reconcile to himself all things, whether on earth or in heaven, by making peace through the blood of the cross."

The majestic description of King Jesus in Colossians 1 gives us a much needed perspective on Luke's story. The man hanging on the cross is "the image of the invisible God . . . the head of the church . . . the beginning . . . the firstborn from the dead." What looks like total defeat is actually God's great victory over sin. The taunting by the religious leaders and the Romans soldiers is ironic and welcome good news – "He saved others; let him save himself . . . If you are the King of the Jews, save yourself!" That's the point – the King, who could have everything and did have everything, gave up everything, including his life on the cross, that we might have new life and everlasting life.

By the same token, Luke's story of Jesus' crucifixion grounds the lofty and majestic titles of King Jesus in the real-world politics and intrigue and struggles of this world. We may wish to reach up to heaven, maybe even to escape this challenging world somehow. But

Luke's story reminds us that God reached down to us when he came to live among us and die for us in the person of Jesus of Nazareth. On this Christ the King Sunday, as we wrap up another church year and look ahead to the season of Advent, we look forward to celebrating the birth of the King and the coming in fullness of the kingdom of God's beloved Son, "in whom we have redemption, the forgiveness of sins."

One of Whitney *Houston's* best songs from the movie, *The Preacher's Wife*, is "Who Would Imagine a King?" Listen to the lyrics:

Mommies and daddies always believe
That their little angels are special indeed
And you could grow up to be anything
But who would imagine a king

A shepherd or teacher is what you could be
Or maybe a fisherman out on the sea
Or maybe a carpenter building things
But who would imagine a king

It was so clear when the wise men arrived
And the angels were singing your name
That the world would be different cause you were alive
That's what heaven stood still to proclaim

One day an angel said quietly
That soon he would bring something special to me
And of all those wonderful gifts he could bring
Who would imagine, who could imagine
Who would imagine a king

That's the point on this Christ the King Sunday. Who would imagine a king who had everything but gave it up for us? Who would imagine a king who loves us so much that he would die for us? Who would imagine a king who had no throne, no private secretaries, no crown jewels, no pomp and pageantry? Who would imagine a king, whose most powerful act – dying on the cross for the forgiveness of sins – would be seen by the world as weakness, foolishness, and total defeat? Who would imagine a king like King Jesus?

To paraphrase King George III to John Adams, "I pray the church doesn't suffer for wont of King Jesus." As we enter into Advent and seek to be faithful disciples of our King, let us work hard to fulfill that prayer.

A Church Full of Zebras and Ostriches
Galatians 5:13-15; Romans 1:1-17

On Friday night, July 29, we had a delightful visit with Dustin and Sherri Ellington and one of their sons, Christopher. The Ellingtons are home on leave from their missionary posting in the southern African country of Zambia. This was our first chance to meet the Ellingtons in person. We hope it won't be the only chance we have to be with them in person. In the meantime, we can keep them in our prayers, as they finish their furlough in the States and as they resume their work at the Justo Mwale Theological University College in Lusaka, Zambia.

Here is part of an e-mail I received from Dustin the day after their visit with us:

> "Dear Phil, We had such a good time with you all last night. How encouraging to see such a large group of people come to the gathering. Sherri and I appreciated the many different conversations we were able to have with people. Thank you again for organizing the event and thanks to everyone for helping to make it happen. We also really like the boys' T shirts and it's nice to have the church directory and look forward to the DVD. May God continue to bless and lead you all in Wallace. Dustin and family"

Dustin and Sherri shared lots of interesting stories and pictures about their life and work in Zambia. At one point in the PowerPoint presentation, Sherri said, "Here are some pictures of what the countryside looks like where we live." One particular slide showed a herd of zebras and a pride of ostriches standing together in a field. Sherri told us, "You often see zebras and ostriches traveling together. They help each other. Ostriches have good eyesight, which zebras lack. Zebras can hear well and have a good sense of smell, which ostriches lack. They work together to protect each other from danger."

In the hallway after the program was finished, Pat Barrow said to me, "Isn't that picture of the zebras and ostriches a good illustration of true Christian community?" Now you know where today's sermon title comes from — and why we have pictures of zebras and ostriches on the front of the bulletin today!

The scientific term for the relationship between zebras and ostriches is "mutualism." "Mutualism" is defined as "a relationship between two species of organisms in which both benefit from the association." The ostrich and zebra both benefit from their mutual relationship by using each other's senses and protecting one another from predators. One article about this "mutualism" between zebras and ostriches had the title "You Look This Way, I'll Listen That Way."

Sherri's picture of the zebras and ostriches, and Pat's comment about true Christian community, got me thinking about the church as the body of Christ, and about our church in particular. The apostle Paul may not have been a biologist, but he certainly understood the concept of "mutualism" when he described the church. Listen to what he has to say about our life together as the body of Christ:

> • "Indeed, the body does not consist of one member but of many...If the whole body were an eye, where would the hearing be? If the whole body were hearing, where would the sense of smell be? As it is, there are many members, yet one body. If one member suffers, all suffer together with it; if one member is honored, all rejoice together with it." (1 Cor. 12:14-26)

> • "For as in one body we have many members, and not all the members have the same function, so we, who are many, are one body in Christ, and individually we are members one of another." (Romans 12:4-5)

> • "Blessed be the God and Father of our Lord Jesus Christ, the Father of mercies and the God of all consolation, who consoles us in all our affliction, so that we may be able to console those who are in any affliction with the consolation with which we ourselves are consoled by God." (2 Cor. 1:3-4)

- "But speaking the truth in love, we must grow up in every way into him who is the head, into Christ, from whom the whole body, joined and knit together by every ligament with which it is equipped, as each part is working properly, promotes the body's growth in building itself up in love." (Ephesians 4:15-16)

- "through love become slaves to one another. For the whole law is summed up in a single commandment, 'You shall love your neighbor as yourself.'" (Galatians 5:13b-14)

Paul usually wrote to people he already knew. His letters to the Galatians, Corinthians, Philippians, and Thessalonians were to folks in churches where Paul had spent some time as their pastor.

That's not the case with Paul's letter to the Christians at Rome. He certainly knew *some* of the members of the church in Rome, because he sends his greetings to them at the end of his letter ("Greet Prisca and Aquila. Greet my beloved Epaenetus. Greet Mary and Andronicus and Junia.").

All in all, Paul calls more than twenty of the church members by name. But he had never been to visit the church in person. He had not established the church in Rome. He was a little bit of an unknown quantity to the Christians in Rome. Paul wanted to make a good impression on them in his introductory letter.

What better way to make a good impression than to compliment the church members on their faith? And that's exactly what Paul does, when he writes, "First, I thank my God through Jesus Christ for all of you, because your faith is proclaimed throughout the world." Paul goes on to assure the Roman Christians that "without ceasing I remember you always in my prayers." My hunch is, Paul would appreciate the church members praying for him, also.

Then Paul lays out his reason for wanting to visit the church members in person: "For I am longing to see you so that I may share with you some spiritual gift to strengthen you . . ." Maybe Paul thought he sounded a little arrogant, since he wasn't the founding pastor of the church, so he continues, "or rather so that we may be mutually encouraged by each other's faith, both yours and mine." I like the translation that Jean Parks shared in Bible study on Wednesday: "I'm eager to encourage you in your faith, but I also want to be encouraged by yours. In this way, each of us will be a blessing to the other." (Rom. 1:12)

Friends, that is the essence of what it means to have a relationship of "mutualism" in our church. Some of us are ostriches — some of us are zebras. When we depend on each other's strengths, when we mutually encourage each other in the faith, we discover that the body of Christ is stronger and our faith is strengthened.

I would never compare myself to the apostle Paul, but I will take a cue from him, and tell you this, who are part of the body of Christ in this place:

> * I thank my God through Jesus Christ for all of you and for your faith;
>
> * I remember you always in my prayers;
>
> * and I am encouraged and strengthened by your faith in Jesus Christ, the faith we hold in common.

I think I have some spiritual gifts to share with you, to strengthen you. I **know** you have spiritual gifts and a faith to share with me and with each other, that will mutually encourage us all. As one writer has put it, "I need encouragement, and so do you. I like to say — Every preacher needs a preacher. . . No believer can make it alone; we need each other. Regardless of how long we have been a Christian or how active in church we have been, we will never be so mature that we can't benefit from the spiritual input of other believers."[1] In his commentary on Paul's letter to the Romans, John Calvin says the same thing about the mutual benefits of sharing our faith and spiritual gifts with one another in the body of Christ, but he is much more blunt: "[Paul] means what he says, too, for there is none so void of gifts in the Church of Christ who cannot in some measure contribute to our spiritual progress. Ill will and pride, however, prevent our deriving such benefit from one another. Such is our superiority and such the intoxicating effect of our stupid boasting, that every one of us despises and disregards others, and so considers that he possesses a sufficient abundance for himself."[2]

All of this talk about "mutualism" and "encouraging one another" in this congregation might sound like we're turning inward and focusing only on ourselves. That's not the point. Instead, our mutual encouragement in the faith — both yours and mine — will strengthen us for the ministry and mission God calls us to do. If you look this way, and I listen that way, and we depend on and draw strength from one another in our common faith in Jesus Christ as Lord, our congregation will be all the better prepared to work together to meet God's call to our congregation.

Such "mutualism" and encouragement and strengthening of the body of Christ won't just happen on its own, however. All of us — ostriches and zebras — need to be intentional in how we develop community in our congregation. One way to develop that deeper sense of community is through small groups. Now, our congregation already has some small groups: Presbyterian Women's circles, Sunday School classes, and the choirs. Members of any of those groups will quickly tell you how much encouragement and support they give and receive in these groups. "The ties that bind" us together as the Wallace Presbyterian Church are strengthened in those groups.

A couple of months ago, I preached a sermon called "Family Ties." In that sermon I talked about the value, importance, and possibilities of more small groups in our congregation. I also extended a general invitation to anyone who might interested in learning more about being in a small group. Well, now some folks who are in an ongoing small group — and who have been mutually encouraged by each other's faith — are inviting you to learn more about the joys and strengths of being part of a small group. You're invited to Nick and Lee Baker's house on Thursday, September 1, at 6:30 p.m. to hear how being part of a small group can strengthen your faith AND how being part of a small group can help you share your spiritual gifts to strengthen other folks in our congregation.

As I was reading for and thinking about today's sermon, I came across a great description of what a small group can mean for your faith and for our congregation. I'd like to share those thoughts with you:

"When we come together for a corporate worship gathering there are certain things we can do well: We can sing worship songs to the Lord, we can listen to the Scriptures expounded, we can greet scores of believers, and we can reach out to unchurched people who come through our doors. But mutual encouragement from each other's faith happens best in smaller groups. In a small group context, we can intimately share our faith struggles and successes. We can comfort one another and bear each other's burdens. We can encourage each other to press on, and in doing so find inspiration in one another's faith."[3]

I thank my God through Jesus Christ for all of you. I thank my God through Jesus Christ that we have a church full of zebras and ostriches. I thank my God through Jesus Christ for the spiritual gifts and encouragement you share with me as your pastor. I thank my God through Jesus Christ for the opportunities God gives us to be mutually encouraged by each other's faith.

If you'll look this way, I'll listen that way. . .

and together, with the power of God's Holy Spirit, we can build up the body of Christ here in the Wallace Presbyterian Church.

NOTES

[1]Keith R. Krell, "Church on a Mission," at www.media1.razorplanet.com.

[2]*Calvin's New Testament Commentaries: The Epistles of Paul to the Romans and Thessalonians*, trans. R. Mackenzie, eds. David W. Torrance and Thomas F. Torrance (Grand Rapids, MI: Wm. B. Eerdmans Publishing Company, 1960), p. 24.

[3]Krell, "Church on a Mission."

When Words Fail Us
Romans 8:18-30

Ann Carter called me and said, "Phil, a plane just flew into the World Trade Center building in New York." I asked, "Ann, what's going on?" "I don't know," she said.

I walked next door to the manse and told Nancy what had happened. We turned on the TV to get an update. A few minutes later, I went back to the church and Cheryl and I put a TV in my study. Nancy came over and the three of us watched the second plane hit the second tower. Then we saw the reporter at the Pentagon cringe as the plane crashed there. Then the report came in about the plane crashing in the field near Shanksville, Pennsylvania. Then, as if things couldn't get any worse, the three of us, along with all of you and millions of other people, watched in disbelief as the Twin Towers collapsed.

If you're old enough to remember the events of 9/11/01, you'll never forget where you were and what you were doing when you heard the news.

A while back, when I noticed that 9/11 would be on a Sunday this year, I started thinking about how we could and would acknowledge the 10th anniversary.

I looked in my sermon files and found the sermon I preached on September 16, 2001, the first Sunday after 9/11. The opening paragraph of that sermon from ten years ago inspired the theme of today's sermon and the rest of this morning's worship service — "When Words Fail Us." I'd like to read that opening paragraph to you now:

What to say? That's the question I have been struggling with since Tuesday as I have thought about this sermon. Really, what is there to say? We've all seen the unbelievable pictures of the airplanes crashing, the World Trade Center towers crumbling, the Pentagon on fire, the jagged gash in the Pennsylvania countryside. We've all seen the incredible agony on the faces of family members and rescue workers. We've been moved to tears by the poignant posters plastered on the New

York walls, with their pictures of the missing, and by the picture of the firefighters raising the American flag on the pile of rubble. We've struggled with the outrage and the anger and the helplessness and the overwhelming sorrow. And now we're starting to hear the stories, as the "1000's of missing" become real individuals — mothers and fathers, wives and husbands, sisters and brothers, aunts and uncles, co-workers and friends. What to say?

Ten years later, as we read the retrospective stories in the paper and online and watch accounts of 9/11 on TV, we may still wonder, "What to say?" That's not to say that, as people of faith, we have nothing to say! But sometimes life overwhelms us and we have trouble finding the right words — or any words — to express how we're feeling.

Sometimes life overwhelms us with its beauty and majesty and joy — and words fail us.

Sometimes life overwhelms us with its tragedy and suffering and challenges — and words fail us.

In the ten years since 9/11, you and I both have had words fail us, in times of joy and in times of sorrow. There have been times when we didn't know what to say to each other. There have been times when it's been hard to know what to say even to God. On this 9/11, ten years later, it might be hard to know exactly what to say.

Consider, then, the ringing assurance and promise of these words from Romans 8: "Likewise the Spirit helps us in our weakness; for we do not know how to pray as we ought, but that very Spirit intercedes with sighs too deep for words. And God, who searches the mind of the Spirit, knows what is the mind of the Spirit, because the Spirit intercedes for the saints according to the will of God." (Romans 8:26-27)

Life presents us with hard questions for which we don't always have the answers. Listen to another paragraph from my sermon on the Sunday after 9/11: *All across our nation this week, people have turned to prayer and worship for strength and support. As people gathered in this sanctuary on Friday at noon for a time of worship and prayers and Scripture, there was great comfort and strength derived from knowing that all across the United States*

— in big cities and in small communities, in ornate cathedrals and relatively plain sanctuaries — people were turning to God for guidance and solace and strength. Gathering for prayer, singing the hymns, hearing the scriptures read — these things don't guarantee that all of our questions will be answered. Rev. Billy Graham admitted as much in his remarks at the National Prayer Service on Friday, when he said that he had never formulated an answer to the question of suffering that he found personally satisfying. But, he said, he has his faith in God. In the face of what has happened this week, **that** *is something to say!*

In the midst of some of the most magnificent words in the Bible, the apostle Paul asks, "What then are we to say about these things? If God is for us, who is against us?" (Romans 8:31) That is Paul's introduction to his soaring affirmation that nothing — absolutely nothing — in all of creation can separate us from the love of God in Christ our Lord. When our words fail us, God's Word stands strong and reminds us of God's promise and power and majesty, even and especially in life's most trying times.

When words fail us, we have the gift of music to lift us up, to express our feelings, to offer a time for reflection and prayer. There is a framed print hanging on the wall of the choir room, right next to the door which we walk out of every Sunday morning as we head to the sanctuary to lead worship. The words are from a German opera house. This is what the print says:

Bach gave us God's Word.
Mozart gave us God's laughter.
Beethoven gave us God's fire.
God gave us music that we might pray without words.

One of my favorite hymns is "When in Our Music God Is Glorified."

When in our music God is glorified,
And adoration leaves no room for pride,
It is as though the whole creation cried: Alleluia!

How often, making music, we have found
A new dimension in the world of sound,
As worship moved us to a more profound
Alleluia!

The rest of today's worship service is intended to move us to a more profound "Alleluia!" through the gift of music. After the July cookout for the Ellingtons, Karla and I sat in the Fellowship Hall and talked about our experiences at the Montreat Worship and Music Conference and the handbell workshop in Minneapolis. Karla said, "I've got this piece of music for the handbell choir to play on 9/11." She described to me how the pictures on the screen and the music of the handbells would provide a time of reflection and meditation on the 10th anniversary of 9/11. I thought, "This is what we need to do."

In just a minute, the handbell choir will play "Prayer for Peace" by Michael Helman. As you listen to the music, you will be able to see images from 9/11 projected on the screen at the front of the sanctuary. The images can be jarring, even ten years later. Let Michael Helman explain in his own words his purpose for writing "Prayer for Peace:"

The events of September 11, 2001, dramatically affected us all. As someone who visits New York City on a regular basis, I truly felt a personal loss. Many times I started my day with a train or ferry ride across the Hudson River to the World Trade Center. Watching the events unfold on television, I felt a strong need to see firsthand what was left of New York's great landmark. My feelings were only heightened as I played for the funeral of a young man killed at the Pentagon on that fateful day. So, at the end of September, I made my pilgrimage to Ground Zero. I was profoundly moved by what I saw that day. No television camera or journalists' words truly captured the destruction and devastation to lower Manhattan.

What could I do to help? What could I do for all those families who lost loved ones, not only in New York, but at the Pentagon and in the air crash in Pennsylvania? I set pen to paper and poured out my feelings and my prayers in music. I hope that others will hear this prayer for world peace and remember not only those who lost their lives on September 11 but also the heroes and heroines who toiled so desperately trying to save lives. The four opening chords of this piece represent the four planes that crashed that day. The chords include all twelve tones of the chromatic scale to symbolize the effect that terrorism has on everyone. My hope is that this composition may be a prayer for an end to terrorism and for peace throughout the world.

Here's how today's service will end. Following the sermon, the handbell choir will play "Prayer for Peace" as images of 9/11 are shown at the front of the sanctuary. When the music is over, there will be a time of silence for all of us to pray and reflect. If words fail you, let the music be your prayer. And remember, "the Spirit helps us in our weakness . . . the Spirit intercedes with sighs too deep for words."

After the time of silence and reflection, our chancel choir will sing Pepper Choplin's song, "Love of the Lord," which he wrote for our 125th anniversary celebration. This magnificent piece of music is based on Romans 8:31-39, which assures us that nothing in life will be able to separate us from the love of God in Christ Jesus our Lord. The choir's song will be today's benediction. Following the benediction, you are invited to remain for more prayer and reflection, if you would like, or you may go ahead and leave the sanctuary.

One more paragraph from my sermon on the Sunday following 9/11. This was the last paragraph. It's just as true today as it was ten years ago: *We gather today as Americans who have been profoundly hurt and affected by Tuesday's terrible events. But first and foremost, we gather today as people who believe in the sovereign God, Creator of heaven and earth, who loved the world so much that he gave his only Son. We gather today, aware of our anger, our outrage, our heartache, our helplessness, struggling with our emotions, anxious about the future, wanting justice to be done. But we also gather as people with whom God has promised to walk — and as people whom God calls "to do justice, to love kindness, and to walk humbly with him."*

What then are we to say about these things? May the gift of this music help us pray without words. May the gift of this music move us to a more profound "Alleluia!" to our God who loves us in Christ Jesus our Lord.

God from A – Z
Titus 2:11-14; Psalm 111

*A*lleluia! Praise the Lord!

*B*ehold the works of the Lord!

*C*ome and worship the Lord with your whole heart!

*D*elight in the goodness of our God.

*E*mbrace God's power and love for our congregation.

*F*ull of honor and majesty is his work,

*G*reat is his name and greatly to be praised.

*H*e has shown his people the power of his works,

*I*n giving them the heritage of the nations.

*J*ust as he promised, our God is gracious and merciful.

*K*eep God's laws with faithfulness and uprightness.

*L*ove describes the kind of God we worship and serve.

*M*anna from heaven he rained down on his people,

*N*ever forgetting his covenant.

O give thanks to the Lord!

*P*raise the Lord!

*Q*uail fed his people in the wilderness.

*R*ighteousness and redemption are our God's,

*S*alvation is ours through him.

*T*rust in God's faithfulness and righteousness,

*U*ntil you come to know his power and greatness.

*V*alue God's name above all other names.

*W*isdom begins when we stand in awe of God's mighty deeds.

e*X*pect great things from our God.

*Y*our works, O God, are faithful and just; all of your precepts are trustworthy.

*Z*eal for God's commandments leads to a good understanding of our God from A – Z.

The psalmist only had twenty-two letters of the Hebrew alphabet to deal with. I had to use twenty-six letters, including such challenges as Q, V, X, and Z!

You can't see it in the English Bible and you can't hear it in the English language, but Psalm 111 was originally written in twenty-two short Hebrew phrases. Each phrase begins with the next letter in the Hebrew alphabet, etc. Biblical scholars call this an "acrostic" psalm.

What took the editors of the New Revised Standard Version one hundred sixty-five words to say — and me, two hundred ten words — the psalmist was able to say in just seventy-two short Hebrew words. As one writer has put it, "In a mere seventy-two words, the psalmist summarizes the whole history of God's deliverance of ancient Israel . . ."[1]

Something else you can't see in the English Bible or hear in the English language is that Psalm 112 is almost a "twin" of Psalm 111. Psalm 112 is also an acrostic psalm, with the same Hebrew alphabetical pattern. One preacher called Psalm 111 "The ABC's of Theology" and Psalm 112 "The ABC's of Anthropology." Psalm 111 is about God: who God is and what God does. Psalm 112 is about us human beings: how we do or do not respond in faith and trust to who God is and what God does.

Suppose someone were to ask you, "Who is God?" How would you answer?

Would you lay out some kind of philosophical argument about God as the first cause of everything there is?

Would you try to describe who God is by contrasting God with what we are? (For example, "We are finite, God is *in*finite.")

Would you shrug your shoulders and throw up your hands and say, "Who knows?"

Or, would you describe God in terms of what God does for his people, by which we find out what kind of God we worship and serve?

"He has gained renown by his wonderful deeds; the Lord is gracious and merciful."

How do we know this? "He provides food for those who fear him . . ."

"Full of honor and majesty is his work, and his righteousness endures forever."

How do we know *this*? "He sent redemption to his people; he has commanded his covenant forever."

"Holy and awesome is his name."

How do we know this? "The works of his hands are faithful and just; all his precepts are trustworthy. They are established forever and ever, to be performed with faithfulness and uprightness."

This week, Nancy and I went to a pastors' lunch at First Presbyterian Church in Jacksonville. As we were getting ready to leave after lunch, I noticed some brochures about FPC on the table in the hallway outside of the Fellowship Hall. Next to the brochures was a stack of pamphlets called "Who Are We Presbyterians?" As I skimmed over the pamphlet, this phrase jumped out at me: "The Presbyterian Church (U.S.A.) is distinctly a confessional church . . ."

What does that mean — "distinctly a confessional church"?

It means that we Presbyterians are moved to say what we believe about God because of what God has done — and continues to do — for us and through us, especially in his Son, Jesus Christ our Lord. As "distinctly a confessional church," the Presbyterian Church (U.S.A.) is in good company with God's people, stretching all the way back to the earliest Hebrew pilgrims in the Sinai wilderness.

When Moses was up on the mountain and God gave him the Ten Commandments, God also had this to say about himself:

"The Lord, the Lord, a God merciful and gracious, slow to anger, and abounding in steadfast love and faithfulness, keeping steadfast love for the thousandth generation, forgiving iniquity and transgression and sin. . ."

That sounds a lot like the confession of faith in Psalm 111, about our God who does wonderful works for his people, including sending redemption and keeping his covenant forever.

That also sounds a lot like the Affirmation of Faith we will use today in worship. Our affirmation will be part of "A Brief Statement of Faith" from our Presbyterian Church (U.S.A.) *Book of Confessions*. That statement of faith has three parts — Jesus Christ, God, and the Holy Spirit — which are framed by doxologies of praise and thanksgiving.

I often ask people, "Why do you think the Brief Statement of Faith begins with the section about Jesus Christ, instead of about God?" Folks always get the point when they say something like, "Well, it's because of and through God's love in Jesus Christ that we know who God is." That's exactly right — what we believe about who God is comes from what God has done for his people through the ages.

Think about what we will confess and affirm about God in a few minutes:

- In sovereign love God created the world good and makes everyone equally in God's image;

- God acts with justice and mercy to redeem creation;

- In everlasting love, the God of Abraham and Sarah chose a covenant people;

- God delivered the children of Israel from the house of bondage;

- Loving us still, God makes us heirs with Christ of the covenant;

- Like a mother who will not forsake her nursing child, like a father who runs to welcome the prodigal home, God is faithful still.

This is who God is.

This is why we give thanks to God with our whole heart.

This is the God we are called to worship and serve and obey.

I have a book on my bookshelf by Eugene Peterson called *Praying with the Psalms: A Year of Daily Prayers and Reflections on the Words of David.* I pulled the book off the shelf the other day and looked up Psalm 111. Surprisingly, he had only one short entry from Psalm 111, for September 12, about v. 10: "The fear of the Lord is the beginning of wisdom; all those who practice it have a good understanding. His praise endures forever."

Peterson's reflection on this verse is worth hearing and thinking about: "Do we think praise is the natural exuberance of the contented person? It is not — it is the thoughtful response of the redeemed. It springs, not from our good feelings, but from God's good acts. We praise God, not when we feel good, but when we realize that God is good."

He also included a prayer for reflection on Psalm 111: "I will remember and observe your goodness through the hours of this day, O God, keeping in mind what you have done faithfully through centuries of redemption, and staying alert to what you presently are doing in the lives of companions in faith. And I will use all I remember and observe to lift praises to you. Amen."[2]

For quite a while now, I have signed my e-mails with this tagline: "Ask yourself this: Where is God already at work in this situation?" I have gotten quite a few comments about that question, and have had some good conversations with people about what it means.

Philip Gladden

Sometimes it's hard to see where God is already at work in the different situations and circumstances of our lives. Psalm 111 reminds us and reassures us that God *is* and **always has been** at work on our behalf.

You often hear the advice, "Count your blessings!" Another way to put it might be to think about God from A – Z. In other words, think about what God has done for us in sending redemption to his people in the person of Jesus Christ, his only Son, our Lord. More than that, instead of just thinking about what God has done, sit down and write a psalm of praise and thanksgiving for what God has done and who God is. Use one of the psalms of David as your guide. Try writing an acrostic psalm, using the letters of the alphabet as your guide. That will really focus your attention.

Then you just might begin to see where God is already at work. Then you might be moved to praise God, as Eugene Peterson puts it in his translation of Psalm 111, "I give thanks to God with everything I've got." We're called to give thanks to God with everything we've got — from A – Z — because God has given us everything he's got from A - Z, "for the grace of God has appeared, bringing salvation to all . . . while we wait for the blessed hope and the manifestation of the glory of our great God and Savior, Jesus Christ." (Titus 2:11, 13)

NOTES

[1]Nancy deClaisse-Walford, "Commentary on Psalm 111," at www.workingpreacher.org.

[2]Eugene H. Peterson, *Praying with the Psalms: A Year of Daily Prayers and Reflections on the Words of David* (San Francisco: HarperSanFrancisco, 1993), for September 12.

Home
Hebrews 10:19-25; Psalm 84

Game 7 of the National League Championship Series . . .

Bottom of the ninth . . . two out . . . home team is at bat, behind 2-1, men on second and third . . .

A trip to the World Series is riding on this game.

The third-string catcher comes to the plate and hits a line-drive single to left field.

One run easily scores and it's 2-2 . . .

and the runner on second, one of the slowest runners in baseball, lumbers down the base path and makes the turn at third.

Some people say the third base coach frantically gave him the STOP signal. The runner says he doesn't remember seeing the signal. He just took off running when he heard the bat hit the ball.

Now it's the future National League Most Valuable Player in left field

against one of the slowest runners in baseball, who is headed home.

The throw is toward the plate, but a little bit wide right.

The runner slides just under the catcher's desperate attempt to tag him out.

The umpire calls the runner SAFE!

The runner has made it home.

As the home team mobs their teammate at home and the fans are going crazy, the announcer shouts over and over, "Braves win! Braves win! Braves win! Braves win! Braves win!"

Philip Gladden

Twenty years ago this October, Sid Bream scored the winning run for the Atlanta Braves against the Pittsburgh Pirates, and the Braves went to their second consecutive World Series. For this long-suffering Braves fan of the late 1960's and through the 1970's and 1980's, who went to see the Braves play when there were sometimes only 1,000 fans in Fulton County Stadium, Sid Bream's run home seemed like it was in slow motion. But he made it there safely. And this Braves fan was jumping up and down and hollering in the upstairs bedroom of the manse on Cleveland Street in Roanoke Rapids, North Carolina!

Before he became the Commissioner of Major League Baseball in 1989, A. Bartlett Giamatti was president of Yale University for eight years, and a professor of comparative literature for a number of years before that. When it rumored that he was being considered for the presidency of Yale, Giamatti, a die-hard Boston Red Sox fan said, "The only thing I ever wanted to be president of was the American League." Instead, he was blessed to become president of the National League in 1986, and commissioner in 1989. Unfortunately, he died of a heart attack after only 154 days in office, at the age of 51.

Shortly after leaving his teaching post to become Yale's president, Bart Giamatti wrote an essay for a Hartford newspaper in which he said, "Baseball is about going home and how hard it is to get there and how driven is our need. It tells us how good home is. Its wisdom says you can go home again but that you cannot stay. The journey must always start once more . . ."[1]

Shortly after becoming commissioner, Bart Giamatti wrote another essay called "The Story of Baseball: You Can Go Home Again." In it, he repeats the theme of "going home," and says that baseball is "the story of going home after having left home; the story of how difficult it is to find the origins one so deeply needs to find." He likens the runner on the basepaths to the journey through life – negotiating the twists and turns and the dangers and threats such as the shortstop or being thrown out at first or getting caught stealing or being stranded far from home on second base. He writes, "To attempt to go home is to go the long way around, to stray and separate in the hope of finding completeness in reunion, freedom in reintegration with those left behind."

Listen to what Bart Giamatti has to say about "home": " 'Home' is an English word virtually impossible to translate into other tongues. No translation catches the associations, the mixture of memory and longing, the sense of security and autonomy and accessibility, the aroma of inclusiveness, of freedom from wariness, that cling to the word 'home' and are absent from 'house' or even 'my house.' Home is a concept, not a place; it is a state of mind where self-definition starts; it is origins — the mix of time and place and smell and weather wherein one first realizes one is an original, perhaps like others, especially those one loves, but discrete, distinct, not to be copied. Home is where one first learned to be separate and it remains in the mind as the place where reunion, if it ever were to occur, would happen."[2]

"Home is where the heart is," wrote Pliny the Elder, a first century A.D. Roman writer.

"There's no place like home. There's no place like home," said Dorothy, as she closed her eyes and clicked her ruby slippers.

"Well, I'll never be a stranger and I'll never be alone. Wherever we're together, that's my home," sang Billy Joel on his 1973 *Piano Man* album.

A few thousand years ago, the psalmist wrote about "going home" when he said, "How lovely is your dwelling place, O Lord of hosts! My soul longs, indeed it faints for the courts of the Lord; my heart and my flesh sing to the living God. Even the sparrow finds a home and the swallow a nest for herself, where she may lay her young, at your altars, O Lord of hosts, my King and my God . . . For a day in your courts is better than a thousand elsewhere. I would rather be a doorkeeper in the house of my God than live in the tents of wickedness." (Psalm 84:1-3, 10)

You can hear Psalm 84 as the song of a faithful pilgrim, slowly making his way down the home stretch to God's holy Temple in Jerusalem. He's going home. He's going to God. He's going to be with his fellow pilgrims to find his place in the courts of the Lord. You can certainly hear Psalm 84 describing a pilgrim walking the twisting, turning, danger-filled path to Zion. You can also hear Psalm 84 as a tale about the pilgrimage of life which leads home. You can hear Psalm 84 as a song about longing for home, as Bart Giamatti wrote, "To attempt to go home is to go the long way around, to stray and separate in the hope of finding completeness in reunion, freedom in reintegration with those left behind." Psalm 84 says, what you find when you get home is the presence of God in the presence of God's people.

It's often said that a newcomer to the South is asked three questions: (1) Where are you from? or Where's home? (2) Who are your people? and (3) Where do you go to church? Those questions are a pretty good description of what it means to be in God's house among God's people.

We talk about our "church family" here at the Wallace Presbyterian Church. We consider this sanctuary to be a special place — "home" — because of whom we meet when we come here and what goes on here when we make it home. When I stand up to lead worship on Sunday morning and look out at all of you, I often think about all of the things we've been through together —— births and deaths, weddings and funerals, good times and bad, special worship services and countless committee meetings, visits by hospital bedsides and singing by the lake at Camp Kirkwood. I think about our church family in this place and how much it means to me. And I think about God who calls us, again and again, to make our way home — and how deep is our need, how much our souls long to be at home with God and one another.

From the second century A.D. writings of Justin Martyr, we have the earliest description of Christians coming together on a weekly basis to hear the scriptures read and a sermon preached, to pray together, to share the bread and wine together and to send it by way of the deacons to those who are absent, and to contribute money to take care of the widows and those who are needy because of sickness. In his book about Sunday worship called *With Glad and Generous Hearts*, William Willimon writes, "You are familiar with this pattern of worship. Two thousand years later, you are still enacting this phenomenon at your church on Sunday morning. This dynamic of gathering, hearing, acting, and scattering in Jesus' name is at the heart of Christian worship, the very center of the Good News. So let us begin with a definition of who you are as a Christian: *A Christian is someone who has heard the call of Jesus to 'follow me.' In obedience to Jesus' invitation, Christians now gather with others who have heard the same invitation in order to listen to Jesus, to speak to him, to eat and drink in his presence, and to celebrate his work in the world. Then we scatter. Having been refreshed and re-created on Sunday, we are now able to live as his disciples in ways that show forth the Good News to others. We are Sunday people.*"[3]

Eleven days ago, the Worship Committee held a training workshop for ushers and greeters. Lee and Curt gave us some very helpful tips about making our church an even more friendly and welcoming place for visitors and guests. We talked about extending hospitality, beginning the minute someone arrives at our church, and welcoming them to our church family. We also talked about how important it is to extend that same hospitality and welcome to *everyone* who comes to our church, both visitors and members. We need to make sure that we welcome and include everyone who comes to God's house to find a home among God's people.

As part of her orientation to Asheville when she got to college a couple of weeks ago, Natalie visited the Thomas Wolfe Homeplace. Of course, he is remembered for his novel, *You Can't Go Home Again*. The story is about George Webber, a new author who writes a book in which he frequently mentions his hometown. Although his book is a national success, George Webber is not very welcome at home because his neighbors are not happy with what he wrote about them and their town.

Webber realizes that "You can't go back home to your family, back home to your childhood . . . back home to the father you have lost and have been looking for, back home to someone who can help you, save you, ease the burden for you, back home to the old forms and systems of things which once seemed everlasting but which are changing all the time--back home to the escapes of Time and Memory."[4]

But Psalm 84 tells us that we *can* go home again — that at the end of our pilgrimage, we can find our home because we can find our God in the midst of God's people. Psalm 84 tells us that when we round third and see home up ahead, we can know with full assurance

Philip Gladden

that God waits there for us, not to tag us out but to welcome us home. And when we have to leave home again to trek through the pilgrimage of the week ahead or of life itself, to run the basepaths (as it were), we can look forward to going home again, in the profoundest sense.

Yes, you *can* go home again. May we always do our best to make the Wallace Presbyterian Church a place where people can be at home with our God and one another, where people can say, "Home is where my heart is," where people can say and really mean it, "There's no place like home."

NOTES

[1] "A Gentleman and a Scholar," at www.sportsillustrated.cnn.com.

[2] A. Bartlett Giamatti, "The Story of Baseball: You Can Go Home Again," April 2, 1989, in *The New York Times* at www.nytimes.com.

[3] William H. Willimon, *With Glad and Generous Hearts: A Personal Look at Sunday Worship* (Nashville: The Upper Room, 1986), p. 18.

[4] Thomas Wolfe, *You Can't Go Home Again*. Quote found at www.goodreads.com/quotes.

Spiritual *and* Religious
Mark 12:28-34; James 1:17-27

One result of having two children in college is that I have learned how to text on my cellphone. I'm not ashamed to admit that before August 2008, I had never sent a text to anyone. However, during parent orientation at the Savannah College of Art and Design, we were advised to learn how to text if we wanted to communicate with our college freshmen. So, I learned and it worked. Now I consider myself a fairly proficient texter.

I must admit, however, that I haven't really gotten into using "textspeak," that highly developed system of abbreviations and acronyms. Occasionally I will shorten a word or two, but I usually take the time to type out an entire message. Sometimes the message I get back requires some decoding.

I came across a helpful resource called "Text speak made easy." Under the heading "Acronyms and Text Messaging for Parents" is this description: "Have you ever watched your children sending or receiving text messages on mobile phones or chatrooms, but can't understand a word of what's being said? Help is at hand with our simple textspeak translator." Some of the abbreviations were familiar — LOL (for Laugh Out Loud), ILU (I Love You), and JK (Just Kidding). Most were new to me. A few of my favorites are: P911 (Parent Alert); POOF (Goodbye); AYTMTB (And You're Telling Me This Because?); and ZZZ (Sleeping, Bored).[1]

Here's an acronym I didn't find in the "textspeak" dictionary: SBNR. That stands for "Spiritual But Not Religious?" Although I couldn't find a reference to SBNR in the textspeak dictionary, there is a website — www.sbnr.org — which ways, "SBNR.org serves the global population of individuals who walk a spiritual path outside traditional religion. This is your home for open source spirituality."[2] SBNR also has a Facebook page.

Is it possible to be "RBNS"? That is, "Religious But Not Spiritual"? Of course it is. The danger is just as great in both camps — "SBNR" and "RBNS." "Spiritual But Not Religious" misses out on the importance of the faith community. "Religious But Not Spiritual" can turn into a dry, demanding legalism or a set of lofty ideas unconnected to the realities of human life and the God who has revealed himself in the person of Jesus of Nazareth.

BJ Gallagher is a blogger for *The Huffington Post*. In numerous articles about "SBNR," she has been cited as saying "she's SBNR because organized religion inevitably degenerates into tussles over power, ego, and money."[3] Well, if SBNR *really* means not tussling over power, ego, and money, I can agree with that. As a religious person who seeks a deeper spiritual relationship with God and God's people, I really have no interest in tussling over power, ego, and money. It's unfortunate that we get caught up in those struggles in the church, among many others, but I'm not convinced that we can or should define "religion" only in those terms.

Well, then, how can or should we define "religion" in a way that honors God, serves our neighbor, and helps us nurture our spiritual relationship with God and neighbor? The Letter of James gives us this definition of "religion": "If any think they are religious, and do not bridle their tongues but deceive their hearts, their religion is worthless. Religion that is pure and undefiled before God, the Father, is this: to care for the orphans and widows in their distress, and to keep oneself unstained by the world." (James 1:26-27)

Here's how Eugene Peterson's translation, *The Message*, says the same thing: "Anyone who sets himself up as 'religious' by talking a good game is self-deceived. This kind of religion is hot air and only hot air. Real religion, the kind that passes muster before God the Father, is this: Reach out to the homeless and loveless in their plight, and guard against corruption from the godless world."[4]

When I was a senior in college, my close friend, Glen, was asked to read a scripture passage of his choosing at the Spring Convocation, where the honors were awarded. A few days before the ceremony, Glen showed me the scripture passage he had picked — Amos 5:21-24 — and asked me, "What do you think?" I told him I thought it was an interesting selection, he was probably going to get a lot of comments, and it was a good choice.

On the day of the convocation, the faculty and seniors processed into the auditorium in the main campus building. There was quite a bit of pomp and circumstance. The ceremony began and, eventually, Glen got up to read his scripture selection:

I hate, I despise your festivals,

and I take no delight in your solemn assemblies.

Even though you offer me your burnt-offerings and grain-offerings,

I will not accept them;

and the offerings of well-being of your fatted animals

I will not look upon.

Take away from me the noise of your songs;

I will not listen to the melody of your harps.

But let justice roll down like waters,

and righteousness like an ever-flowing stream.

You could have heard a pin drop in the auditorium! But it was an appropriate message and reminder to the community gathered there that day. What is the point of our "solemn assemblies," our "offerings," our "songs and melodies," if we don't work for justice and righteousness? What was true for that academic gathering is just as true, even more true, for our *religious* gathering here today and every Sunday. It's possible to be "religious" — to have solemn assemblies and give offerings and sing songs — without getting involved in the messier, more demanding work for justice and righteousness. It's also possible to be "spiritual" — to have some vague appreciation for a higher power or to pick and choose form different religious/spiritual traditions — without committing yourself to the religious community, even with all of its quirks and idiosyncrasies that come from the church being made up of human beings.

I suppose it depends on what we mean by "religion." Our small group is reading Eugene Peterson's book, *A Long Obedience in the Same Direction: Discipleship in an Instant Society.* Just this week we talked about the chapter about what it means to be "servants" as religious people who follow Jesus Christ. Here's what Peterson says:

"Too often we think of religion as a far-off, mysteriously run bureaucracy to which we apply for assistance when we feel the need. We go to a local branch office and direct the clerk (sometimes called the pastor) to fill out our order for God. Then we go home and wait for God to be delivered to us according to the specifications that we have set down. But this is not the way it works. And if we thought about it for two consecutive minutes, we would not want it to work that way. If God is God at all, he must know more about our needs than we do; if God is God at all, he must be more in touch with the reality of our thoughts, our emotions, our bodies than we are; if God is God at all, he must have a more comprehensive grasp of the interrelations in our families and communities and nations than we do . . . If we want to understand God the way he really is, we must look to the place of authority — to Scripture and to Jesus Christ."[5]

Three friends decided to go deer hunting together. One was a lawyer, one a doctor, and the other a preacher.

As they were walking, along came a big buck. The three friends shot simultaneously. Immediately the buck dropped to the ground and all three rushed up to see how big it actually was.

Upon reaching the buck, they found out it was dead, but had only one bullet hole. Thus, a debate following concerning whose buck it was.

A few minutes later a game officer came by and asked what the problem was. The doctor told him their reason for their debate. The game officer told them he would take a look and tell them who shot it.

Within a few seconds, the game officer said with much confidence, "The pastor shot the buck!" They all wondered how he knew that so quickly.

The officer said, "Easy! The bullet went in one ear and out the other."

Listen to how *The Message* counsels us to make the connection between "spiritual" and "religious": *Don't fool yourselves into thinking that you are a listener when you are anything but, letting the Word go in one ear and out the other. Act on what you hear! Those who hear and don't act are like those who glance in the mirror, walk away, and two minutes later have no idea who they are, what they look like. But whoever catches a glimpse of the revealed counsel of God — the free life! — even out of the corner of his eye, and sticks with it, is no distracted scatterbrain but a man or woman of action. That person will find delight and affirmation in the action."*[6]

When one of the scribes asked Jesus, "Which commandment is the first of all?" Jesus answered, "You shall love the Lord your God with all your heart, and with all your soul, and with all your mind, and with all your strength. The second is this, 'You shall love your neighbor as yourself.'" (Mark 12: 28-34) Jesus binds our relationship with God so closely with our relationship with one another, it's impossible to separate them.

That scribe was one astute religious leader, for he wisely said, " 'to love God with all the heart, and with all the understanding, and with all the strength,' and 'to love one's neighbor as oneself,' — this is much more important than all whole burnt offerings and sacrifices." (Mark 12:33)

Let's not neglect our religion — our theology, our worship, our community — at the expense of our spirituality. The life of discipleship — "a long obedience in the same direction" — is more than just "me and Jesus, and everything's OK." Our spiritual life, our relationship with God through Jesus Christ, is expressed in our religious life as a community of faith. What people are looking for — indeed, what *God* is looking for — is a direct connection between our spirituality and our religiosity, a direct connection between our love for God and our love for our neighbors.

I am in the midst of teaching "Introduction to the Study of Religion" to a group of Religion majors at the University of Mount Olive. In Chapter One of our textbook, you find the authors' definition of religion: "Religion signifies those ways of viewing the world that refer to (1) a notion of sacred reality (2) made manifest in human experience (3) in such a way as to produce long-lasting ways of thinking, feeling, and acting (4) with respect to problems of ordering and understanding existence."[7]

That's a good, academic definition of "religion." What does it mean for you and me as disciples of Jesus Christ and for us as the Wallace Presbyterian Church, a part of the body of Christ? It means: We believe in a personal God whom we worship and serve, who has made himself known to us in his only Son Jesus Christ, who died for our sins, who calls us to "a long obedience in the same direction" as disciples, as we seek to live a meaningful and purposeful life of worship, service, and love in God's name and for the people our God has created.

So, the question shouldn't be RUSBNR? ("Are You Spiritual But Not Religious?")

The question should be RUSARITPAUSBGTF? ("Are You Spiritual *and* Religious In the Pure and Undefiled Sense Before God the Father?")

IHS ("I Hope So")

GBWY ("God Be With You")

PTL ("Praise the Lord!")

AMEN ("Amen.")

NOTES

[1] www.talktalk.com.uk/community/textspeak-p1.html.

[2] www.sbnr.org.

[3] I found references in numerous articles, but have taken this quotation from www.schott.blogs.nytimes.com/2010/06/16/sbnr/

[4] Eugene H. Peterson, *The Message: The Bible in Contemporary Language* (Colorado Springs, CO: NavPress, 2002), p. 2203.

[5] Eugene H. Peterson, *A Long Obedience in the Same Direction: Discipleship in an Instant Society* (Downers Grove, IL: IVP Books), pp. 62-63.

[6] Peterson, *The Message*, p. 2203.

[7] Cunningham, Lawrence S. and John Kelsay, *The Sacred Quest: An Invitation to the Study of Religion, Fifth Edition* (Boston: Prentice Hall, 2010), p. 21.

Thank You, Jesus!
Jeremiah 31:31-34; Hebrews 10:11-18

One of the clues on "Jeopardy!" the other night was a picture of barefoot young man dressed in a robe who was tacking a piece of paper on a wooden door. Alex Trebek said something like, "This young German monk of the 16th century nailed his 95 theses to the castle door at Wittenberg." One of the three contestants asked the correct question: "Who was Martin Luther?"

Listen to what Martin Luther himself had to say about his experience in the Augustinian monastery: "I was a good monk, and I kept the rule of my order so strictly that I may say that if ever a monk got to heaven by his monkery it was I. All my brothers in the monastery who knew me will bear me out. If I had kept on any longer, I should have killed myself with vigils, prayers, reading, and other work."[1]

Johann von Staupitz probably would have said "Amen!" to Luther's description of his zealous "monkery." Von Staupitz was the vicar of the monastery where Luther served, and became Luther's confessor. According to the younger monk, Luther, "If it had not been for Dr. Staupitz, I should have sunk in hell." At the time, Luther struggled with an overwhelming sense of personal sin. It is said that he tried to confess everything he had ever done wrong, only to return to his monk's cell and agonize when he would remember more sins he had forgotten to confess. At least once he made confession for six hours without stopping. Imagine what poor Dr. Staupitz was thinking!

Actually, at one point Dr. Staupitz said, "I don't understand it!" when Martin Luther confessed to him that he had come to hate God. Luther was so afraid of Jesus Christ as judge, he could not accept God's grace and forgiveness. Dr. Staupitz kept urging the young monk to keep thinking on God's grace and to surrender to God's love in Jesus Christ. Eventually, as a result of his study and teaching of Romans and Galatians, Martin Luther experienced the life-changing revelation that "the righteous shall live by faith."

How many of us wrestle with the same questions and doubts as the young monk, Martin Luther? How many of us live our lives afraid that God is out to get us, waiting for the chance to zap us for our sins? How many of us live our lives burdened by the guilt of accumulated sins, able to acknowledge intellectually that Jesus died for our sins on the cross, but shackled by the nagging feeling that we will never measure up to God's standards of righteousness?

In his book, *Christian Doctrine*, Shirley Guthrie tells the story about a little boy who went to a revival meeting. He had grown up in a Christian home and in the church, but that night he heard something he had never heard before.

The preacher held up a dirty glass. "See this glass? That's you. Filthy, stained with sin, inside and outside."

The preacher picked up a hammer. "This hammer is the righteousness of God. It is the instrument of God's wrath against sinners. God's justice can be satisfied only by punishing and destroying people whose lives are filled with vileness and corruption."

The preacher put the glass on the pulpit and slowly, deliberately drew back the hammer. He took deadly aim, and with all his might let the blow fall.

But a miracle happened! At the last moment he covered the glass with a pan. The hammer struck with a crash that echoed through that hushed church. The preacher held up the untouched glass with one hand and the mangled pan with the other.

"Jesus Christ died for your sins. He took the punishment that ought to have fallen on you. He satisfied the righteousness of God so that you might go free if you believe in him."

When the boy went to bed that night, he could not sleep. Meditating on what he had seen and heard, he decided that he was terribly *afraid* of God. But could he *love* such a God? He could love Jesus, who had sacrificed himself for him. But how could he love a God who wanted to "get" everyone and was only kept from doing it because Jesus got in the way? The thought crossed the boy's mind that he could only hate such a hammer-swinging God who had to be bought off at such a terrible price. But he quickly dismissed the thought. That very God might read his mind and punish him.

Some other thoughts also troubled the boy. Despite what the preacher said about the righteousness of God, is it really right to punish one person for what other people do? And granted that he was a pretty bad boy sometimes, was he really all that bad? Did he really deserve to *die*? Was he really so sinful that God had to *kill* Jesus to make up for what he had done?

Finally, he wondered what good it had all done in the end. The glass had escaped begin smashed to bits, but nothing had really changed. After the drama was over, it was still just as dirty as it was before. Even if Jesus did save him from God, how did Jesus' sacrifice help him to be a different person?[2]

Contrast that little boy's scared reaction and his troubling questions with the approach Lucy takes in a *Peanuts* cartoon. Lucy walks up to Charlie Brown, holding a piece of paper and a pen, and says to him, "Here, sign this. It absolves me from all blame." Then Lucy goes to see the piano-playing Schroeder with the same paper. "Here, sign this. It absolves me from all blame." Lucy visits all of the kids in the Peanuts gang, with the same piece of paper and the same demand. Finally, Lucy meets up with her little brother, Linus. "Here, sign this. It absolves me from all blame." As Lucy walks away, Linus says, "Well, that must be a nice document to have."

Two very different approaches to the life of faith:

We can live our Christian lives the way the young monk, Martin Luther, and the little boy who went to the revival did – scared of God, constantly trying to measure up, being frustrated that we never can, and being driven to despair . . .

OR . . . we can use our Christian faith the way Lucy used her piece of paper that she claimed absolved her from all blame. We can do whatever we want because, you know, Jesus paid it all. Jesus took care of our forgiveness on the cross. We're absolved of all guilt for whatever we do, so what difference does it make what we do?

I know a whole lot more Christians who struggle with Martin Luther's dilemma of constantly trying to please God than I know Christians who are so cavalier about how they live. We hear the good news of the gospel: "In Jesus Christ, your sins are forgiven," but we forget to live as if it's true. Somehow we convince ourselves that Christ's death on the cross must surely need some kind of a boost, so we offer up our sacrifices of good works, good intentions, going to church, being involved. When we offer these sacrifices over and over again to try to earn God's love and merit God's forgiveness, we eventually find out that it is never enough. We're like the priest who stood daily in the temple, serving and repeatedly presenting the same sacrifices, which can never remove sins.

But the Letter to the Hebrews shows us another way and tells us this good news: "For by a single offering he has perfected for all time those who are sanctified." The author of Hebrews quotes those tender and overwhelmingly welcome words of God to his people, "I will remember their sins and their lawless deeds no more." Then the writer of Hebrews adds, "Where there is forgiveness of these, there is no longer any offering for sin."

The Letter to the Hebrews reminds us that the cross of Jesus Christ stands at the center of our Christian faith, our Christian proclamation, and our Christian lives. The apostle Paul put it this way, "For I decided to know nothing among you except Jesus Christ, and him crucified." (1 Cor. 2:2) The cross of Jesus Christ towers over all of history and all of our lives as the symbol of God's righteous judgment AND of God's merciful love. If we focus only on God's judgment in the cross, and forget God's love expressed in Jesus' death for our sins, we'll always have a picture of God as the hammer-swinging God who is out to get us – and Jesus will be the one who has to "save" us from that hammer-swinging God.

But that's not what the good news of Jesus Christ tells us. The cross of Jesus Christ doesn't save us from *God – God* saves us from sin with the cross of Jesus Christ. The cross holds us to account in our lives, but the cross also offers us hope and freedom to live for God and for one another. That's what changes our good works from sacrifices offered to try to earn God's love and merit God's grace into offerings that we bring in grateful response to God's love and grace in Jesus Christ, our Lord.

This week we take a day to offer our thanksgiving to God for all that God does for us. Our prayers will include thanksgiving for life and health and food – for family and friends – for freedom and the blessings of this land. All are appropriate prayers.

Perhaps as we give thanks on Thursday, we can also think about what sorts of sacrifices or offerings we bring before God. Will we live our lives trying to appease God? Trying to win God's favor? Trying to avoid the wrath of a hammer-swinging, angry God? Burdened by guilt and weighed down by "every sin that clings so closely"?

Or will we live our lives in joy, assured of God's love and forgiveness in the cross of Jesus Christ – free from guilt, free to live for God, free to do justice, free to love kindness, and free to walk humbly with our God? As the Letter to the Hebrews tells us, Christ has "offered for all time a single sacrifice for sins . . . Where there is forgiveness of these, there is no longer any offering for sin." Above all else, that is reason for thanksgiving this week!

When Martin Luther realized that God's righteousness comes to us as a gift in faith, he said, "When I understood that and when the concept of justification by faith alone burst through into my mind, suddenly it was like the doors of paradise swung open and I walked through."

I tell you: In the name of Jesus Christ, we are forgiven.

Thank you, Jesus!

NOTES

[1] www.prayerfoundation.org/favoritemonks/favorite_monks_martin_luther.htm

[2] Shirley C. Guthrie, *Christian Doctrine: Revised Edition* (Louisville: Westminster/John Knox Press, 1994), pp. 250-251.

Don't You Worry 'Bout A Thing
Matthew 6:25-34; Philippians 4:4-7

If Stevie Wonder had written Philippians 4:6, he might have said, "Don't you worry 'bout a thing..."

If Bobby McFerrin had written Philippians 4:6, he might have said, "Don't worry, be happy!"

If Alfred E. Neuman of MAD magazine had written Philippians 4:6, he might have said, "What, me worry?"

But it was the Apostle Paul who wrote Philippians 4:6, and he **did** say, "Do not worry about anything, but in everything by prayer and supplication with thanksgiving let your requests be made known to God."

But that is *so* hard to do, isn't it? Instead of not worrying about anything, but in everything letting our requests be made known to God, we find ourselves anxious and, as a result, something like the person described in this little poem by Shel Silverstein. It's called "God's Wheel."

God says to me with a kind of smile,

"Hey, how would you like to be God awhile

And steer the world?"

"Okay," says I, "I'll give it a try.

Where do I set?

How much do I get?

What time is lunch?

When can I quit?"

"Gimme back that wheel," says God.

"I don't think you're quite ready yet."

Four years ago, as part of The Pastor as Spiritual Guide program, I led a six-week Lenten study of Henri Nouwen's book, *Making All Things New: An Invitation to the Spiritual Life*. Nouwen was a Catholic priest who discovered his calling to serve as senior pastor of L'Arche Daybreak in Toronto. L'Arche Daybreak is a community where men and women with disabilities and their assistants create a home for one another. Henri Nouwen, who died in 1996, is well-known for his writings about developing our spiritual lives in the midst of restless and hectic lives.

Nouwen's point of departure in *Making All Things New* is Jesus' words, "Do not worry." He concludes the first section of his book, which he calls "All These Other Things," with these thoughts:

"One of the most notable characteristics of worrying is that it fragments our lives. The many things to do, to think about, to plan for, the many people to remember, to visit, or to talk with, the many causes to attack or defend, all these pull us apart and make us lose our center. Worrying causes us to be 'all over the place,' but seldom at home. One way to express the spiritual crisis of our time is to say that most of us have an address but cannot be found there. We know where we belong, but we keep being pulled away in many directions, as if we were still homeless. 'All these other things' keep demanding our attention. They lead us so far from home that we eventually forget our true address, that is, the place where we can be addressed.

Jesus responds to this condition of being filled yet unfulfilled, very busy yet unconnected, all over the place yet never at home. He wants to bring us to the place where we belong. But his call to live a spiritual life can only be heard when we are willing honestly to confess our own homeless and worrying existence and recognize its fragmenting effect on our daily life. Only then can a desire for our true home develop. It is of this desire that Jesus speaks when he says, 'Do not worry . . . Set your hearts on his kingdom first . . . and all these other things will be given you as well.'"[1]

"Only then can a desire for our true home develop." Years ago, the psalmist expressed that very same desire when he wrote, "As a deer longs for flowing streams, so my soul longs for you, O God. My soul thirsts for God, for the living God." (Psalm 42:1-2)

Philip Gladden

With the same desire but with different words taken from another psalm, we were called to worship this morning:

We desire food in the wilderness.
We thirst for living water in the barren desert.
We long for nourishment,
for relationship,
for comfort,
for joy,
for peace.
We long for God.
We long for God.
And so we have come.
And so we wait.
And so we praise.

In our fast-paced, busy, and preoccupied modern lives, it might seem unrealistic, foolhardy, even dangerous to heed Jesus' advice, "Do not worry about your life" and Paul's admonition, "Do not worry about anything." Are we supposed to go through life with no regard for what might happen? Are we supposed to adopt a "hands-off" approach to life? Are we supposed to be unconcerned about what happens to us and the people around us? For people who are steeped in taking responsibility for our lives and the world around us, Jesus' and Paul's words certainly confront us as a challenge. At face value, they seem to call us to a life of irresponsibility at worst, a life of naiveté at best. However, there is another way to hear what Jesus and Paul are telling us, a much more positive approach to the spiritual life, when our soul longs for God, thirsts for the living God.

When I was in seminary, learning how to prepare sermons, we were taught to do "word studies" as we translated the scripture texts from the original Hebrew and Greek languages. The point of a word study is to see how a particular key word in your scripture passage is used in other biblical passages. This word study is often very helpful in determining how best to translate (or not translate) the particular word.

For example, in the fourteen New Testament verses we heard read this morning, the word for "being anxious" or "worrying" shows up seven times. Obviously, that word is important for our understanding of what Jesus and Paul mean.

The Greek word for "anxious" and "worrying" can also mean "care for" and "be concerned about." As one biblical commentator has said, "Obviously there is appropriate as well as inappropriate anxiety." From a "positive" point of view, this word means "to be concerned about," as when Paul talks about the church being the body of Christ, and the members having "the same care for one another" (1 Cor. 12:25) or when he tells the Philippians that he and Timothy are "genuinely concerned for your welfare" (Phil. 2:20). But there is also a "negative" connotation of the word, such as when Jesus tells Martha that she is worried and distracted by many things, so much so that she misses out on the more important thing, listening to Jesus (Luke 10:38-42)

The worrying and being anxious about many things that makes us miss out on the more important things is what both Jesus and Paul are warning us about. We live in an anxious time, and there seems to be plenty to be anxious about. But there's a big difference between "being anxious" and "being concerned."

Several years ago, I must have been pretty anxious, because I have a collection of sayings about anxiety and worrying written in my quote journal. Here they are:

"People gather bundles of sticks to build bridges they never cross."
(Author unknown)

"For peace of mind, resign as general manager of the universe."
(Author unknown)

"Do not be afraid of tomorrow; for God is already there."
(Author unknown)

"Don't cross that bridge until you get to it, or else you'll have to pay the toll twice."
(Bill Browder, member WPC)

"I've had a lot of worries in my life, most of which never happened."

"I have been through some terrible things in my life, some of which actually happened."
(Mark Twain)

"Worrying does not take away tomorrow's troubles, just today's peace."
(Author unknown)

"Don't trouble trouble until trouble troubles you."
(Overheard at a presbytery council meeting)

"Yes, there is a God. It is not you."
(Sign at Little Chapel on the Boardwalk Presbyterian Church, Wrightsville Beach, NC)

"Don't you worry 'bout a thing!" If it were simply up to us, that might be some of the worst advice we could be given. It's kind of like someone telling you, "Don't think about anything!" Inevitably, you think about *everything*. "Don't you worry 'bout a thing!" If nothing else, when left to our own devices, we might well be anxious about the fact that we can't *not worry* 'bout a thing!

But neither Paul nor Jesus leaves us to our own devices as the people of God and followers of Jesus Christ.

Jesus says, "Therefore, I tell you, do not worry about your life . . ." He also says, "indeed your heavenly Father knows that you need all these things. But strive first for the kingdom of God and his righteousness, and all these things will be given to you as well."

Paul says, "Do not worry about anything . . ." He also says, "but in everything by prayer and supplication with thanksgiving let your requests be made known to God. And the peace of God, which surpasses all understanding, will guard your hearts and your minds in Christ Jesus."

Concerned for – caring about? Yes! Anxious, worrying? No! Is it all up to us? By no means!

"Don't worry about your life" and "Do not worry about anything" are other ways of saying what we've heard the last two weeks: "For surely I know the plans I have for you, says the Lord, plans for your welfare and not for harm, to give you a future with hope" (Jeremiah 29:11) and "We know that all things work together for good for those who love God, who are called according to his purpose." (Romans 8:28)

In 1941, William Wilson, the co-founder of Alcoholics Anonymous, became aware of a prayer by the great Reformed theologian, Reinhold Niebuhr. The AA staff printed copies and started distributing them to AA members. The Serenity Prayer has been a part of AA ever since. While many people may be very familiar with the opening lines, perhaps you've never heard the entire prayer. Niebuhr's words certainly reflect the spirit of Jesus' and Paul's encouragement not to worry, but to trust God's goodness in all things.

God, give me grace to accept with serenity
the things that cannot be changed,
courage to change the things
which should be changed,
and the wisdom to distinguish
the one from the other.
Living one day at a time,
enjoying one moment at a time.
Accepting hardship as a pathway to peace,
taking, as Jesus did,
this sinful world as it is,
not as I would have it,
trusting that you will make all things right,
if I surrender to your will,
so that I may be reasonably happy in this life,
and supremely happy with you forever in the next.
Amen.

Our small group has begun to re-read Henri Nouwen's book. As we were talking the other night about Nouwen's thoughts on worry and anxiety and God's call to "be at home," I made the comment that I don't worry nearly as much as I used to, when worries and anxiety could almost be debilitating. Somebody asked what made the difference. I gave a one-word answer, "Surrender." I think that's what Jesus and Paul both are talking about when they encourage us not to worry, not to be anxious, but to put our trust in God who knows that we "need all these things."

That's why I have another quote in my quote journal, this one from Father Timothy Kavenaugh, the main character of Jan Karon's books about his life and ministry in the small town of Mitford. In the book, *Home to Holly Springs*, Father Tim says, "I surrendered my life to him. That was the breakthrough. Before that, I was merely a man with an agenda. After that, I was God's man and it was his agenda. It changed everything."[2]

Amen and amen!

NOTES

[1] Henri J. M. Nouwen, *Making All Things New: An Invitation to the Spiritual Life* (New York: HarperCollins Publishers, 1981), pp. 36-37.

[2] Jan Karon, *Home to Holly Springs* (New York: Penguin Group, 2007).

Famous Last Words
Numbers 6:22-27; 2 Corinthians 13:11-13

Famous last words:

Watch this!

What does this button do?

Trust me, I know what I'm doing!

Then there is the inscription on the large white crypt in the Key West 1847 cemetery that says, "I told you I was sick."

Comedian Rodney Dangerfield's grave marker says, "There goes the neighborhood."

Famous last words:

How about the tombstone that reads, "Here lies an atheist. All dressed up and nowhere to go"?

Winston Churchill expressed his desire to be buried in the cemetery of St. Martin's Church in Bladon, England. His tombstone inscription says, "I am ready to meet my Maker. Whether my Maker is prepared for the great ordeal of meeting me is another matter."

Martin Luther King, Jr.'s final words in his famous "I Have A Dream" speech grace his final resting place in Atlanta: "Free at last, free at last! Thank God Almighty, I'm free at last!"

As he lay dying on Sunday, May 10, 1863, after being shot by one of his own men at the Battle of Chancellorsville, General Thomas "Stonewall" Jackson weakly said, "It is the Lord's Day; my wish is fulfilled. I have always desired to die on Sunday." His last words were, "Let us cross over the river, and rest under the shade of the tree."

Philip Gladden

Having survived a horrendous carriage accident and an assassination attempt on the night President Abraham Lincoln was killed, Secretary of State William Seward was on his deathbed on October 10, 1872. When his children asked him if he had any deathbed advice to give, he quietly whispered to his daughter-in-law, "Love one another."

Famous last words . . . they can be spontaneous, well-thought out, humorous, pithy, sarcastic, meaningful.

Perhaps there have never been – nor ever will be – any more poignant or significant or welcome famous last words than those uttered by Jesus as he hung on the cross: "He said, 'It is finished.' Then he bowed his head and gave up his spirit." (John 19:30)

Here are some other last words:

"The grace of our Lord Jesus Christ be with you." (Romans 16:20)

"The grace of our Lord Jesus Christ be with you. My love be with all of you in Christ Jesus." (1 Corinthians 16:23-24)

"May the grace of our Lord Jesus Christ be with your spirits, brothers and sisters." (Galatians 6:18)

"Grace be with all who have an undying love for our Lord Jesus Christ." (Ephesians 6:24)

"The grace of the Lord Jesus Christ be with your spirit." (Philippians 4:23)

"Grace be with you." (Colossians 4:18)

"The grace of our Lord Jesus Christ be with you." (1 Thessalonians 5:28)

"The grace of our Lord Jesus Christ be with all of you." (2 Thessalonians 3:18)

"Grace be with you." (1 Timothy 6:21)

"The Lord be with your Spirit. Grace be with you." (2 Timothy 4:22)

"Grace be with all of you." (Titus 3:15)

"The grace of the Lord Jesus Christ be with your spirit." (Philemon 25)

These are the last words of the Apostle Paul. They aren't "last words" in the sense of deathbed professions. Instead, they are his signature sign-off to his letters to the churches at Rome, Corinth, Galatians, Ephesus, Philippi, Colossae, Thessalonica, and to his fellow believers Timothy, Titus, and Philemon.

Tradition has it that Paul was martyred – beheaded – during the reign of Emperor Nero around the mid-60's A.D. Tradition also says that Paul was buried in Rome. Excavations began in 2002 on a crypt under a basilica in Rome, long thought to be Paul's burial place. A probe of the crypt showed incense, pieces of blue and purple linen, and bone fragments. Archeologists performed radiocarbon tests on the bone fragments in the crypt and found them to date from the 1st or 2nd century A.D. In 2009, Pope Benedict XVI announced the results of the testing and said the test results were consistent with the traditional claim that the crypt was the final resting place of the Apostle Paul.

The inscription on the sarcophagus reads "Paul apostle martyr."

I wonder if Paul had any say-so in what was carved on his tombstone. The simple words "Paul apostle martyr" are consistent with how Paul typically identifies himself in his letters to the different churches – "a servant of Jesus Christ, called to be an apostle; called to be an apostle of Christ Jesus by the will of God; an apostle – sent neither by human commission nor from human authorities, but through Jesus Christ and God the Father, who raised him from the dead; a prisoner of Christ Jesus."

However, it seems likely that if Paul had had his druthers, he would have had these famous last words written on his gravestone for all to see:

Philip Gladden

"The grace of our Lord Jesus Christ,
the love of God,
and the communion of the Holy Spirit
be with all of you."

Those are the last words I leave with you every Sunday morning in worship. I don't remember when I started using Paul's famous last words as the conclusion of my weekly benediction. What I do know is, now that I've been using them for so long, I don't think I'll ever stop using them. From time to time, I'll pronounce additional words of benediction that, in one way or another, tie in with the message of the morning's sermon. But I'll always end the benediction with that trinitarian formula about the grace of Jesus Christ, the love of God, and the communion of the Holy Spirit.

As I said, I don't remember when I started using Paul's benediction on a weekly basis, but I do know **why** I started using the words. The reason is really quite simple. In my opinion, you can't improve upon the depth of meaning and the significance for our Christian lives as expressed in these last words. As I was working on this sermon, it struck me that whenever I lead my final worship service – one day far in the future! – these famous last words of Paul will most likely be the very last words I speak as a worship leader among God's people. You can't get any better than that!

In June 1983, the two largest Presbyterian denominations in the United States reunited in Atlanta, after one hundred twenty years of division, dating to the Civil War. Our own Elder Joe Eaddy was a commissioner from Wilmington Presbytery at that historic General Assembly.

In the years following reunion, the Presbyterian Church (U.S.A.) found it important to say "This is what we believe!" As a result, a new "Brief Statement of Faith" was adopted by the church. True to our historic Christian and Reformed beliefs, the creedal statement is trinitarian in form. The confession of faith begins with this profession:

In life and in death we belong to God.
    Through the grace of our Lord Jesus Christ,

>   the love of God,
>   and the communion of the Holy Spirit,
>   we trust in the one triune God, the Holy One of Israel,
>   whom alone we worship and serve.

That certainly ought to sound familiar this morning. The rest of the statement of faith follows that outline:

We trust in Jesus Christ . . .

We trust in God . . .

We trust in God the Holy Spirit . . .

The final line of the Brief Statement of Faith can be said or sung:

Glory be to the Father, and to the Son, and to the Holy Spirit. Amen.

Why, if we are so used to saying, "Father, Son, and Holy Spirit," do we end each worship service with "Son, Father, and Holy Spirit"? Why would Paul, of all people, leave us with this benediction in this order?

Well, as someone has put it so well, "Behind the grace of the Lord Jesus Christ, which is known as an observable event in history, stands the love of God, which, though commended in time in the action and especially in the death of Jesus, is an eternal fact." In other words, we come to know God's love for us through the grace of Jesus Christ (especially in his death on the cross) and that love energizes us and calls us out through the power of God's Holy Spirit to be the people God wants us to be in this world.

In light of the "eternal fact" of God's love and the blessing of God's grace through Jesus Christ by the power of God's Holy Spirit, we can hear these "famous last words" as the beginning of our call to the Christian life of service and worship and thanksgiving.

If my weekly benediction is nothing more than the pretty bow on the package at 12 noon, then we won't take God's power and promise with us during the week, to face the challenges and meet the opportunities that inevitably will come our way as followers of Jesus Christ.

If we hear Paul's "famous last words" as nothing more than a catchy motto or slogan, with no truth or power for our own lives and for our church, we will be deaf to God's ongoing call to follow Jesus Christ as Lord and Savior. But if we hear Paul's "famous last words" and take them to heart, we can trust God to help us live as faithful servants of the Lord Jesus Christ.

There are certainly many variations of Paul's "famous last words."

As I was preparing for Elizabeth's and Jeffrey's wedding service, I looked back over other wedding ceremonies and came across this good expansion of Paul's benediction:

The grace of Christ attend you,
   the love of God surround you,
     the Holy Spirit keep you,
that you may live in faith,
        abound in hope,
         and grow in love,
           both now and forevermore. Amen.

That's it! This benediction – this "good word" – gives us the assurance that, as we walk out of the doors of this sanctuary, God's grace, love, and power go with us, now and always.

Over the years, many people have shared their reasons for becoming a part of this church family at the Wallace Presbyterian Church. The #1 reason, consistently, is the sense of welcome and belonging "from the minute I walked in the door."

You never know what impact words might have on someone. Lee Woodard has frequently shared that Paul's "famous last words" are the reason he and his family became a part of this church family. Early on, as they were visiting with us, Lee heard the benediction from 2 Corinthians 13:13 – his favorite Bible verse – and thought, "This is the place for us."

In his book, *A Long Obedience in the Same Direction*, Eugene Peterson writes about our Christian lives, "The truth of God explained their lives, the grace of God fulfilled their lives, the forgiveness of God renewed their lives, the love of God blessed their lives." That's a good commentary on Paul's benediction. These are life-changing, life-affirming, life-giving words of grace, love, and fellowship.

I've never really given much thought to what my "last words" will be. I doubt they will be, in any sense, "famous." But, upon reflection, how could you do better than these "famous last words"?

The grace of the Lord Jesus Christ, the love of God, and the communion of the Holy Spirit be with all of you. Amen.

What Does God Want from Me?
Romans 12:1-2; Micah 6:1-8

Please take a hymnbook and turn to hymn #357, "O Master, Let Me Walk with Thee."

Look at the name of the person who wrote the words to this song. You'll find his name in the top, left-hand corner, just beneath the hymn title. "Washington Gladden"

When we would sing "O Master, Let Me Walk with Thee" from the old, red Presbyterian hymnbook when I was a kid, my dad used to nudge me, point to the name, and say, "We're related to him!" Actually, we're not, although sometimes I wish I could claim more than just a shared name with Washington.

When I was a student at Union Presbyterian Seminary, a church history professor named Dr. James Smylie used to stop me on campus and say, "Gladden, Gladden. Are you related to Washington Gladden?" No matter how many times I told Dr. Smylie "No," he would ask me again and again. I told that story to a classmate named Will, who took several classes with Dr. Smylie. One day Will told me Dr. Smylie was lecturing about Washington Gladden in class. Will raised his hand and asked, "Gladden, Gladden. Is he related to Phil Gladden?" Dr. Smylie didn't ask me that question any more – that is, until we had graduated, been out in the church for three and a half years, and then returned to campus for me to begin my graduate work. One day I saw Dr. Smylie on campus. He welcomed me back and then said, "Have I ever asked you if you're related to Washington Gladden?"

Here are just a few of Washington Gladden's activities:

* served as a Congregational minister for almost 5o years (1866-1914), thirty-two of which were as pastor of the First Congregational Church in Columbus, Ohio;

* was a leading member of the Progressive Movement and served two years as a member of the Columbus, Ohio city council;

* served as the religious editor of the *New York Independent* and helped expose the political corruption of Boss Tweed;

* advocated the application of "Christian law" to public issues, including labor disputes and unions; was a charter member of the American Economic Association;

* helped to promote modernist views in interpreting scripture and theology;

* was vice-president, then president, of the American Missionary Association;

* began speaking out against segregation after visiting with W.E.B DuBois at Atlanta University and being shocked at the treatment of blacks in the South;

* served as moderator of the National Council of Congregational Churches;

* was considered for the presidency of Ohio State University until he lost the chance because of a run-in with the American Protective Society.[1]

Washington Gladden is considered one of the founders and early leaders of what is known as the "Social Gospel." The "Social Gospel" was a Protestant religious movement that peaked in North America in the early 20th century. According to one source, "The movement applied Christian ethics to social problems, especially issues of social justice such as economic inequality, poverty, alcoholism, crime, racial tensions, slums, bad hygiene, child labor, inadequate labor unions, poor schools, and the danger of war. Theologically, the Social Gospel sought to put into practice the phrase in the Lord's Prayer (Matthew 6:10): 'Thy kingdom come, Thy will be done on earth as it is in heaven.'"[2]

Washington Gladden's life and career, with his involvement in the Social Gospel movement, is a good illustration of the ongoing and age-hold debate among Christians, "What is the purpose of the Church?"

It should be no surprise that opinions have and do range from one end of the spectrum to the other. On the one hand, you have Christians who say the Church's purpose is first, foremost, primarily, and *only* the preaching of the gospel and the saving of souls. On the other hand, you have Christians who say the Church's purpose is to be engaged in and to work to bring about changes in society and culture.

Critics of the first position say that kind of Christian faith is far too private, that it focuses only on "Jesus and me." Critics of the second position say that kind of Christian faith is nothing more than social work or political activism.

This classic, ongoing debate about faith and works is as relevant today as it was in the 8th century B.C., when the prophet Micah brought God's Word to bear on Israel's faith and national life, and in the 1st century A.D., when Paul wrote to the Christians in Rome, the capital city of the superpower empire, about what it means to live as a faithful Christian.

Listen again to what Micah the prophet has to say to the people of Israel, who wonder how to live faithfully with their God: "He has told you, O mortal, what is good; and what does the Lord require of you but to do justice, and to love kindness, and to walk humbly with your God?" (Micah 6:8)

Listen again to what the apostle Paul has to say to believers in the church at Rome: "I appeal to you therefore, brothers and sisters, by the mercies of God, to present your bodies as a living sacrifice, holy and acceptable to God, which is your spiritual worship. Do not be conformed to this world, but be transformed by the renewing of your minds, so that you may discern what is the will of God — what is good and acceptable and perfect." (Romans 12:1-2)

At this time of year, our church traditionally focuses on Stewardship. One important part of stewardship is how we will financially support our ministries, missions, and outreach. Next Sunday morning, all of you are invited and encouraged to come to the Fellowship Hall at 10:00 a.m. for a Stewardship Celebration. The elders and I and our session committees will have displays set up around the room that will help you learn more about and celebrate the wonderful things God is helping us do here at the Wallace Presbyterian Church.

The purpose of next Sunday's Stewardship Celebration is not *just* to educate the congregation about the financial requirements of being the Wallace Presbyterian Church. The Stewardship Celebration is a way for all of us to think about the question asked in today's sermon title: "What does God want from me?"

I hope and pray that everything we do here at the Wallace Presbyterian Church is always for the praise of and to the glory of the God who redeemed us in Jesus Christ, who has saved us from our sin, and who calls us to a new way of living as his people. I also hope and pray that what we do here at the Wallace Presbyterian Church will always help us fulfill the "Great Ends of the Church," which we Presbyterians have traditionally held up as an integral part of the mission of the church. The six "Great Ends of the Church" are (1) the proclamation of the gospel for the salvation of humankind; (2) the shelter, nurture, and spiritual fellowship of the children of God; (3) the maintenance of divine worship; (4) the preservation of the truth; (5) the promotion of social righteousness; and (6) the exhibition of the Kingdom of Heaven to the world.

It's a debate as old as the Letter of James in the New Testament, which says, "Show me your faith apart from your works, and I by my works will show you my faith." It's a debate as old as the Protestant Reformation and the beginnings of our Reformed, Presbyterian tradition, when John Calvin set out to establish a covenant community in Geneva, Switzerland, and encouraged citizens to be faithful Christians and involved, informed, and educated citizens. It's a debate as old as the history of missions, as denominations and mission co-workers determine how best to share the good news of Jesus Christ as well as address the pressing social concerns of brothers and sisters around the world. And it's a debate as contemporary and relevant as the church's involvement in the Civil Rights movement in the 1950's and 1960's, and the role of people of faith in the Moral Monday protests at the capitol in Raleigh.

But perhaps it's a debate that sets up a false dichotomy — **either** the gospel **or** social involvement. Are we called only to come to this safe place we call the sanctuary and worship God, and yet let it have no effect whatsoever on how we conduct ourselves in our businesses, in our schools, and in the public arena? Are we called only to "do good works" and address the ills of society, without any sort of theological underpinnings of faith in the living God who calls us to do justice, to love kindness, to walk humbly with our God, to present ourselves (our whole selves) as a living sacrifice, holy and acceptable to God?

One thing I appreciate about being a Presbyterian Christian is the oft-quoted idea that "our faith is always personal, but never private." In other words, Presbyterians have a long history of bringing their faith to bear on the communities in which they live and of getting involved in public policy. That's not to say it's easy, or without its controversies. Our Presbyterian Church (U.S.A.) has an Advisory Committee on Social Witness Policy, which is charged with helping the church study and act on pressing moral challenges of the day. Perhaps you'll appreciate what the committee's website says about a life of faith *and* action: "The testimony of a Presbyterian is not simply a personal witness to the saving love of God in Jesus Christ. A Reformed testimony includes a public, corporate witness to the good news found in Jesus Christ for both church and society. The history of the Reformed movement suggests that it is tough enough to witness privately, person-to-person, for the faith. It can be tougher to witness publicly and corporately in a manner which makes clear the gospel call to justice and the vision of a beloved, inclusive community."[3]

The prophet Micah was speaking on behalf of God to people who had strayed from God's ways, despite God's gracious and faithful love and care. When they asked God, "What can we do? What rituals can we perform? What can we give you to make things right? What do you want from us?" God said, "to do justice, to love kindness, and to walk humbly with me." When one of the religious leaders asked Jesus, "What is the greatest commandment?" Jesus didn't give him a list of ritual acts and a set of instructions. He said, "Love the Lord your God with all your heart, and with all your soul, and with all your mind, and with all your strength. Love your neighbor as yourself." (Mark 12:30-31)

At our Tuesday Morning SonRise worship services recently, we have had some words to consider as we gather for worship. Last Tuesday I shared this thought by Rodney Burton: "Worship is not about the posture of your body; worship is about the posture of your heart." The posture of our body covers all of the rituals and traditions and ways of doing things around here. They're not unimportant, but we have to be careful that we don't make our ways of doing things more important than our worship and praise of God and our service to God and our neighbor in doing justice, loving kindness, and walking with God.

A few years ago, I tried a new Christian discipline as a way to hear God's Word afresh in my life. Someone suggested that I pick a psalm and rewrite it in my own words, maintaining the original thought of the psalm while letting it and hearing it speak to my own situation. I tried that for a while and, then, I got away from the practice. Last Monday I pulled out the little journal my kids had given me, which I used to write in, and read some of the psalms I had (re-)written. For what's it worth, here's my re-write of Psalm 50:1-15, 23. It's funny I should read this, which I wrote almost five years ago, as I was beginning a week's work on a sermon about what it means to worship and serve God and to live a faithful Christian life:

God Almighty calls the whole earth all day long, from sunrise to sunset.

God's glory shines more gloriously than that sun that rises and sets.

God is not going to keep his silence; and his speech takes precedence over all. Everybody hears.

God comes to judge, and this is what he has to say: "Get everybody together, all of those who bind themselves to me by their worship."

Then God lets us know where we stand: "I see and hear your worship. I will not get after you for the way you worship me. I know your traditions, 'how you've always done it,' your sense of order and propriety. You see, I don't need any of those things. I don't really want any of those things.

*Instead, I want your hearts, your thanksgivings, your prayers — I want **you**, not your rituals and practices.*

I made you, I know you. I promise you this — when you are in trouble, call on me and I will save you. You will praise and worship and glorify my name.

Do you want to know how to honor me? Bring your hearts full of thanksgiving as your worship. This sacrifice of thanksgiving will set you on the right path with me.

I will show you my salvation!"

God calls you and me and our church to do justice, to love kindness, and to walk in faith with our God. God calls you and me and our church to present ourselves as living sacrifices, holy and acceptable to God, which is our spiritual worship.

May God always grant you and me and our church the grace, wisdom, courage, and love to share the good news of Jesus Christ **and** to work to make a difference in our community and in our world — always to the glory of God!

NOTES

[1] www.en.wikipedia.org/wiki/Washington_Gladden

[2] www.en.wikipedia.org/wiki/Social_gospel

[3] www.presbyterianmission.org/ministries/acswp/about-acswp/

It's Go Time!
Ephesians 1:2-14; Matthew 28:16-20

"It's go time!"

That was the title and theme of Mrs. Janice Wynn's baccalaureate sermon last Sunday night at Wallace Rose Hill High School.

"It's go time! It's go time to put into practice what you have learned in your thirteen years of school — whether you're going on to college, to serve in the military, or to enter the workforce. It's go time to remember who taught you what you know and helped you get where you are today. It's go time to do new things, but don't forget that all us are here for you, always."

"It's go time!"

That is the theme of Jesus' Great Commission to his disciples on the mountaintop in Galilee.

"All authority in heaven and on earth has been given to me. **Go** therefore and make disciples of all nations, baptizing them in the name of the Father and of the Son and of the Holy Spirit, and teaching them to obey everything that I have commanded you. And remember, I am with you always, to the end of the age." (Matthew 28:18-20)

"It's go time! Go, and put into practice what you have learned from me. Make disciples of all the people. Show them what it means to live as my followers. Baptize them in the mighty name of God and welcome them to a new life. Teach them everything you've learned from me. And don't forget — I am ***always*** with you."

On this happy occasion when we baptize Leah Katherine and Amelia Grace, it's go time! A few minutes ago I asked you to remember and renew your own baptisms. By doing so, you recall Jesus' call in your life to be his faithful disciple and God's promise to give you everything you need to do what Jesus Christ asks you to do.

After years and years of reading the Great Commission story in Matthew 28, I had an eye-opening experience this week. This just goes to show how God's Word is always the *living Word*. Jesus tells his disciples (then and now), "Go therefore and make disciples of all nations . . ." Jesus doesn't say, "Go therefore and *save* all nations . . ." Salvation is God's work alone. Discipling and sharing our faith with other people so they can experience God's salvation — that is our calling.

If the idea of discipling "all nations" is too daunting, let's narrow it down a little bit. Think about the questions Andrew and Mary Kate answered as they presented their daughters for baptism. Two in particular asked them about their commitment to "disciple" their girls and to teach them about God:

Do you now unreservedly promise, in humble reliance upon God's grace, to set before Amelia and Leah an example of the new life in Christ?

Do you promise to pray with and for them and to bring them up in the knowledge and love of God?

Now, think about the promises you made as part of the baptismal service:

Do we, the members of this congregation, in the name of the whole Church of Jesus Christ, undertake with Andrew and Mary Kate the Christian nurture of Amelia and Leah, so that in due time they may confess faith in Jesus Christ as Lord and Savior?

Will we endeavor by our example and fellowship to strengthen their family ties with the household of God?

Every one of these questions has "action verbs" — set before; pray with and for them; bring them up; undertake; confess; endeavor; strengthen. Every one of Jesus' instructions to his disciples (then and now) has "action verbs" — go; make; baptize; teach; remember.

This baptism Sunday is also Trinity Sunday on the church calendar.

We began by being called to worship God our Creator who calls us all, Christ our risen Savior who guides us all, and the Holy Spirit who moves us to action.

We praised God with our opening hymn: "Baptized in water, Sealed by the Spirit, Marked with the sign of Christ, our King; Born of the Spirit, We are God's children, Joyfully now God's praises we sing."

In grateful response to God's grace and forgiveness through Jesus Christ, we sang "Glory be to the Father, and to the Son, and to the Holy Ghost."

We affirmed our faith with believers through the centuries: "I believe in God the Father Almighty, Maker of heaven and earth, and in Jesus Christ his only Son our Lord. I believe in the Holy Ghost."

I put water on Leah's and Amelia's heads and said, "Child of the covenant, I baptize you in the name of the Father and of the Son and of the Holy Spirit."

We asked for God's illumination as we listen to God's Word, "through Jesus Christ, the Word made flesh, who was raised and now reigns in the power of your Holy Spirit."

We heard Jesus' command to baptize "in the name of the Father and of the Son and of the Holy Spirit."

We will sing our thanksgiving to God for his wonderful gifts and say, "Praise Father, Son, and Holy Ghost."

And, as happens every Sunday morning, we will be sent out with these words of blessing: "The grace of the Lord Jesus Christ, the love of God, and the communion of the Holy Spirit be with all of you."

We don't extol the virtues of some "Greater Being" or "First Principle."

We don't sign a consent form, simply agreeing intellectually with a set of theological ideas about an ultimate source.

We don't gather to worship some "Unknown God" who may or may not love us, who may or may not be involved with us, who may or may not make himself known to us, who may or may not have a purpose for our lives and for this world.

No, on this baptism and Trinity Sunday, there's a reason we sing and pray and praise and proclaim "one God in three ***persons***." "Here we are to worship, here we are to bow down, here we are to say that you're our God. You're altogether lovely, altogether worthy, altogether wonderful to us."

A "First Principle" doesn't say, "I am with you always, to the end of the age."

A mere intellectual assent to some dogma won't give us the passion and the gifts we need to go out in Jesus' name and do what he calls us to do.

An "Unknown God" who may or may not have a purpose for our lives and our world will not send us out to make disciples and to love in his name.

As someone has said, when we follow Jesus Christ, we are not converted to a philosophy, but to a unique way of living together in the Messiah's community.

And living together in the Messiah's community means going, making disciples, baptizing, teaching, remembering, loving, giving, praising, worshiping . . .

This week I read a wonderful sermon by Dr. James B. Lemler, pastor of the Christ Church Episcopal in Greenwich, Connecticut. His sermon title was "Blah, Blah, Blah, Blah . . . Love." He ended his sermon with this story about a family in the church, who discussed his Sunday sermon over lunch.

"I had a couple of parents telling me the story about their family's Sunday morning experience of a sermon that I had preached. They had gone home and during Sunday lunch were talking about my sermon (something that warms the heart of a pastor to be sure). In the midst of their conversation, the second-grade daughter sitting at the table chimed in. "Oh, Father Lemler's sermons, they're always the same. You know . . . blah, blah, blah . . . love." Well I was amused and thought to myself, "Hey, this little girl really got it . . . the message, the repetition, the core, the redundancy."

Dr. Lemler says, "And so it is with the Holy Trinity . . . the message, the repetition, the core, the redundancy. Over and over again . . . "Blah, blah, blah, love . . ."

God the Creator . . . I love you and give you life.

God the Redeemer . . . I love you and embrace you in that love forever.

God the Spirit . . . I love you and warm your heart and your soul with my love.

Blah, blah, blah, love . . . I welcome you to that love. I enfold you in that love. I hold you forever and ever in that love.

And for our part . . . we are called to believe it. We are called to proclaim it. We are called to invite people into it. We are called to embrace and be embraced by it.

Blah, blah, blah . . . love . . . In the name of the Father and of the Son and of the Holy Spirit."[1]

And to that let me add, "It's go time!"

Go . . . believe, proclaim, invite, embrace, be embraced, live, witness, disciple, teach . . . love.

In the name of the Father and of the Son and of the Holy Spirit.

NOTES

[1] James B. Lemler, "Blah, Blah, Blah, Blah . . . Love," Matthew 28:16-20, at www.day1.org.

The Crosses of Lent

A Cruciform Church
Colossians 1:15-20; Hebrews 12:1-2

How many crosses are there in the sanctuary?

That's what I asked the confirmation group Sunday afternoon as we spent most of our time in here talking about how and why we worship God. The young people walked around and found the Bible on the lectern, the pulpit, the communion table, the baptismal font, and the organ and piano. We talked about **why** those things are **where** they are in the sanctuary. Then I asked them, "How many crosses are there in the sanctuary?" Before they got up and started looking, though, I told them, "By the way, I don't know the answer to my question! See how many you can find."

Right away some of them pointed to the big cross that hangs above the choir (which was donated in 1967 in memory of Dr. John D. Robinson). They found crosses on the cloths or paraments that hang on the pulpit and lectern. Last Sunday afternoon, the cloths were white for Transfiguration Sunday; today they are purple for the season of Lent. Cameron said, "There's a cross on the Christian flag and there's a cross on another flag in the vestibule." Colby pointed out the Presbyterian Church (USA) symbol on his confirmation notebook he had brought into the sanctuary. That symbol is printed in the upper left hand corner on the front page of today's bulletin. Notice how our church symbol is made up of many different symbols, all of which combine to form a central cross. Colby then held up a hymnbook and said, "There's a cross on each of the hymnbooks in here." (That's one reason I didn't know the answer to the question I asked them!)

Then Anna Grace said, "The church is shaped like a cross." While some of the others were asking "What do you mean?" I said, "I was hoping nobody would see that so I could tell y'all about it. Anna Grace, how did you know that?" She said, "You talked about it once in LOGOS." Anna Grace is right — this sanctuary is shaped something like a cross, with the long aisle leading up to the cross bar before the front pews and the chancel area as the top of the cross. If you could float above the pews, you'd have an easier time seeing the cross-shaped pattern.

The "cruciform" or "cross-shaped" architecture of churches dates back many centuries. The symbols in and the architecture of this church remind us of the central place of the cross of Jesus Christ in our faith, in our Christian lives, and in the mission of this congregation. But, to be truly a cruciform church, we must pay attention to more than just pulpit cloths, hymnbooks, Christian flags, and beautiful crosses we hang on the wall.

What does it mean to be a cruciform church? Frederick Dale Bruner writes, " 'Point to Christ!' — that is the rock of the church. 'Follow Christ!' — that is the cement of the church, the substance that takes the rock and joins it to Christ the cornerstone to form the building of God. Rocks without cement are rock piles; cement without rocks is formless. Jesus Christ and the cross of Jesus Christ are the twin building blocks of the church. . . How does a church become a church? Jesus will build his church wherever his disciples faithfully speak of him as the divine and crucified Christ and wherever they faithfully follow him in self-denying obedience. . . The consequences will surely be that the church will redouble her devotion, first of all, to sacred doctrine, whose chief concern is the right witness to Jesus Christ in the church, and then also, as zealously and as soberly, she will devote herself to the ethical obedience of Jesus in the world."[1]

Jesus said to his disciples, "If any want to become my followers, let them deny themselves and take up their cross daily and follow me."

"A cross to bear . . ." Bum knees? A difficult boss? An estranged relationship? A boring job? Poor health? Persistent financial troubles? These may all be hard things to bear in life, but they're not what Jesus is talking about when he says, "Let them deny themselves and take up their cross daily and follow me." Dietrich Bonhoeffer, who was no stranger to suffering for Christ and was hanged by the Nazis just days before the Allies liberated the prison camp where he was held, wrote in his book, *The Cost of Discipleship*, that "the cross is not adversity, nor the harshness of fate, but suffering coming solely from our commitment to Jesus Christ." He also wrote, "When a disciple picks up his or her own cross, it is actually Christ himself who is thereby found."

During this Lenten season, the sermons will be about "The Crosses of Lent." You will find the sermon texts for the next six Sundays printed in today's bulletin and in the February and March newsletters. The sermons will not be about the many different designs of the cross (although that is an interesting topic, in and of itself). Rather, the sermons will be based on Gospel lessons and the writings of the apostle Paul, who told the Christians at Corinth, "For I decided to know nothing among you except Jesus Christ, and him crucified." (1 Corinthians 2:2)

Thursday afternoon I took a PostIt note in to Cheryl with a note about the Food Pantry. When I walked in her office, she looked at the PostIt note in my hand and said, "Oh no, not another sermon title!" I understood why she said that — I had already given her three different titles for today's sermon. Here are the eight possibilities I worked with: Take Up Your Cross Daily; Christ on the Cross; The Crucified Lord; The Church Beneath the Cross; Discipleship and the Cross; The "Must" of Suffering; The Way of the Cross; and, finally, A Cruciform Church. One of these other titles may yet show up in the next six weeks.

For the most part, we Presbyterians don't have a long history of Ash Wednesday observances and practices. On Wednesday of this week, instead of going somewhere and having ashes wiped on my head in the form of a cross, I pulled a book off of the shelf and began to read Dietrich Bonhoeffer's *Meditations on the Cross*. You may remember that Bonhoeffer was a German pastor who resisted the claims of Adolph Hitler in the 1930's. Pastor Bonhoeffer turned down an offer of safety in England or the United States and chose to remain with his people in the German Confessing Church. He was martyred at the age of 39 at the hands of the Nazis.

The blurb on the back of the book says, "The cross and resurrection, suffering, and overcoming death were central themes in Dietrich Bonhoeffer's theological work. Throughout his life, he focused on these themes, trying to disclose their relevance for human life and actions and to answer the question 'What does it mean to be a Christian?'"

Let me share a few of Bonhoeffer's thoughts on the cross of Jesus Christ and what it means for us as Christians and our church:

* "We want Jesus as the visibly resurrected one, as the splendid, transfigured Jesus. We want his visible power and glory, and we no longer want to return to the cross, to believing against all appearances, to suffering in faith." (p. 4)

* "The call to discipleship occurs here in connection with Jesus' announcement of suffering." (p. 11)

* ". . . from its very inception the church itself has taken offense at the suffering Christ. It neither wants such a Lord nor does it, as the Church of Christ, want its Lord to force upon it the law of suffering." (p. 12)

* "Discipleship as commitment to the person of Jesus Christ places the disciple under the law of Christ, that is, under the cross." (p. 12)

* "Self-denial means knowing only Christ, and no longer oneself. It means seeing only Christ, who goes ahead of us, and no longer the path that is too difficult for us. Again, self-denial is saying only: He goes ahead of us; hold fast to him." (p. 13)

* ". . .those who lose their life in discipleship, in bearing the cross, will find it again in discipleship itself, in the community of the cross with Christ. The opposite of discipleship is to be ashamed of Christ, of the cross, and to take offense at the cross." (p. 16)

* "By following under the cross the congregation of Jesus Christ represents the world before God." (p. 17)[2]

Many of those thoughts are taken from Bonhoeffer's book, *The Cost of Discipleship*, in which you will find one of his most famous quotations: "When Christ calls a man, he bids him come and die."

At lunch on Thursday, Nancy asked me, "What did you do this morning?" I answered, "I worked on my sermon, more or less."

Then I paused and said, "Well, actually I spent a lot of time trying to get up the nerve to write my sermon." In light of what Jesus told his disciples about what it means and what is required to follow him, in light of what Dietrich Bonhoeffer wrote about the cross of Jesus Christ and how he lived and died beneath the cross of Jesus, I was actually nervous about writing this sermon. Do I take up my cross daily and follow Jesus? Am I willing to lose my life for Jesus' sake? Am I ashamed of Jesus and his words when push comes to shove?

And what about our church? Do we spend too much of our time trying to "save our life" rather than losing our life as a community for Jesus' sake? How do we take up our cross daily as a church — actively serving Jesus Christ in Wallace and beyond, even if it means suffering and shame? Reformed and Presbyterian Christians have historically referred to the preaching of God's Word and the right administration of the sacraments as marks of the true church. The great reformer, Martin Luther, who surely would have agreed with those two marks, also counted suffering among the signs of the real church.

Lent is traditionally a season of spiritual introspection and taking stock of your relationship with God through Jesus Christ. If we're honest in our Lenten reflections, we have to admit that we usually want to save our lives rather than lose them, even for Jesus' sake. If we're honest, we have to admit we'd rather not and, many times, we don't take up our crosses daily and follow Jesus. If we're honest, we have to confess that the idea of serving a crucified Lord sometimes is either scary or ludicrous.

And yet . . . and yet, Jesus calls us and says, "Take up your cross and follow me." It is precisely **because** Jesus went to his own cross for us that we can even, for a minute, think about taking up our own cross and following him. Have you ever considered the irony, that one of the cruelest forms of death has become the greatest symbol of faith? Frederick Buechner writes, "A six-pointed star, a crescent moon, a lotus — the symbols of other religions suggest beauty and light. The symbol of Christianity is an instrument of death. It suggests, at the very least, hope."[3]

In some Christian traditions and churches, a crucifer walks ahead of the minister or priest and other worship leaders as they process into the sanctuary for worship. The crucifer holds the cross of Christ high in the air.

We don't have a crucifer in the Wallace Presbyterian Church. In a sense, however, we are **all** crucifers. As we will sing in our closing hymn, "All newborn servants of the Crucified bear on their brow the seal of Christ who died. Lift high the cross, the love of Christ proclaim till all the world adore his sacred name."

Our crucified and risen Lord and Savior Jesus Christ is calling us to be a cruciform church, not just in our church architecture and the symbols in our sanctuary, but especially in the lives we live, by the witness we bear, and in the mission we take to our community and the world.

NOTES

[1]Frederick Dale Bruner, *Matthew, Volume 2: The Churchbook, Matthew 13-28* (Dallas: Word Publishing, 1990), pp. 587, 599.

[2]All quotations are taken from *Dietrich Bonhoeffer: Meditations on the Cross,* Manfred Weber, ed. (Louisville: Westminster John Knox Press1998.

[3]Frederick Buechner, *Wishful Thinking: A Seeker's ABC* (HarperOne: 1993).

Jesus Keeps Showing Up
John 20:1-18; John 20:19-31

It was late on a hot August afternoon in North Myrtle Beach. The pastor was walking across the church lawn toward his office and looking at the long line of traffic on Highway 17. It had been a long day and he was looking forward to getting home for the evening.

Then he noticed the young man coming toward him from the highway. He was wearing tan slacks, a bright green golf shirt, and tennis shoes. He was carrying a small canvas bag. "Great," thought the preacher, "this is just what I need after the day I've had. Somebody looking for money, for a meal, for a motel room for the night."

The pastor decided to meet the young man on the front steps of the church. He was prepared to control the situation, but the young man spoke first. "Hello, you're the pastor, right? That's your name on the sign out front?" The pastor was a little bit irritated by the young man's cheerfulness and familiarity, and he immediately said, "Yes. What can I do for you?"

"What can you do?" the young man asked. "Nothing. That is, no more than you are already doing." For some reason, that just irritated the pastor even more. "Look, what do you want? I'm rather busy right now." The young man replied, "I don't need anything. I just wanted to drop by and say hello, to tell you how much I appreciate what you do."

The pastor was trying his best to evaluate the situation and to figure out if the young man posed any kind of threat. "Well," he said, "that's good of you. But who are you? I didn't get your name."

"Jesus Christ."

For some reason, the pastor wasn't really surprised to hear the young man say that. He'd heard just about everything from people over the years. "Look, are you trying to be funny?" But the young man said, "No. Does that strike you as funny? I know you've had a long day. All I wanted to do was to stop by and tell you, face to face, how much I appreciate what you're doing here. I know it's not easy." Then the young man continued, "This isn't the easiest place to serve. But the church looks good and you have done a good job."

The pastor just stood there with his mouth open and nodded.

Then the young man asked, "Do you read the Bible? Are there any questions you have about it? Anything you don't understand?" The pastor couldn't believe it when he heard himself saying, "Yes, I read the Bible, as often as I can. I suppose everybody has questions about it."

"But do you *enjoy* the Bible?" The pastor said, "Yes, I like it, yes."

"Thank you," said the young man.

The pastor asked, "Look, if you're Jesus, where are you going?"

The young man said, "Akron, Ohio." When the pastor said, "You've got to be kidding. Why Akron, Ohio?" the young man replied, "Business, you know, usual stuff." Then he put his hand on the pastor's shoulder and said, "I know you're busy and I don't want to keep you. I just wanted to stop by and say thanks."

The pastor just stared at the young man. "You don't want anything? You don't need something?" "No, no thanks," said the young man, "keep up the good work. Don't be discouraged." Then the young man turned and walked back toward Highway 17. He turned once and waved at the pastor, who sort of half-waved in return.

"Guess who I just talked to," the pastor said to his wife, as she stood there with a cup of coffee in her hands. He told her the whole story. "I hope you didn't cooperate with him," she said. "You didn't encourage him, did you? You mean you just stood there talking with him?"

The pastor said, "What was I supposed to do? I'm seen stranger people in North Myrtle Beach. Jesus himself said stranger things."

Philip Gladden

His wife went back into the kitchen. A few minutes later, she came back with a cup of coffee for her husband. "If he was Jesus, then why was he going to Akron, Ohio?"[1]

Jesus keeps showing up!

That seems to be a pretty obvious Easter Sunday message. In more formal, theological, liturgical language, we proclaim, "Christ is risen! He is risen indeed!" But what that means is, if we **really** believe that Jesus Christ has been raised up from the dead, never to die again, then he will keep showing up, even or especially at the most unexpected times in our lives.

The disciples huddled in that locked room on the evening of the first Easter Sunday might have been as surprised and skeptical and incredulous as the pastor in North Myrtle Beach to meet Jesus. Peter and John had already visited the empty tomb. Mary Magdalene had already announced to the disciples, "I have seen the Lord!" and told them the things Jesus had said to her.

But, do you think they were prepared to meet Jesus there in that locked room? Sure, their reaction was different from the skeptical North Myrtle Beach pastor's reaction. The disciples rejoiced when they saw the Lord. What most of them had only heard about from Peter, John, and Mary they now experienced for themselves, firsthand — Jesus is alive and in their midst!

But for whatever reason, Thomas missed out on meeting Jesus that Easter evening. Imagine the other disciples saying to Thomas, "Guess who we just talked to." When Thomas asks, "Who?" they tell him, "We have seen the Lord!" Now, the pastor's wife said, "I hope you didn't cooperate with him. You didn't encourage him, did you? You mean you just stood there talking with him?" Obviously that's not what Thomas said to his fellow disciples, but he did say, "Unless I see the mark of the nails in his hands, and put my finger in the mark of the nails and my hand in his side, I will not believe." (John 20:25)

Poor Thomas — he doesn't ask for anything the other disciples haven't already received, to see Jesus face to face, to see his wounds and be convinced that Jesus is really alive. After all, Jesus himself showed the other ten disciples his hands and his side without them even asking. Besides that, Thomas makes *the* basic and ultimate confession of faith when he says, "My Lord and My God!"

And yet, 2000 years later, Thomas isn't remembered as "Thomas the disciple" or "Thomas the believer" or "Thomas the confessor" or "Thomas the faithful" or even "Thomas the Twin." No, 2000 years later, we still talk about "Doubting Thomas." But when Thomas actually got what he thought he wanted — "Then [Jesus] said to Thomas, 'Put your finger here and see my hands. Reach out your hand and put it in my side" — Thomas suddenly realized he no longer needed that kind of "proof." As someone has said, this story about Thomas moves him *and* us from belief in the resurrection to faith in the risen Lord.

Jesus keeps showing up!

The risen Lord showed up at the tomb and called Mary by name. (John 20:16)

The risen Lord stood in the midst of his disciples who were hiding out because they were afraid, and he said to them (three times), "Peace be with you." (John 20:19-29)

The risen Lord walked along the road to Emmaus with two of his followers and led them in a Bible study they would never forget. (Luke 24:25-27)

The risen Lord took bread and broke it and gave it to them and their eyes were opened and they recognized him. (Luke 24:30-31)

Jesus keeps showing up!

On this Easter Sunday, if we believe that Jesus has been raised from the dead and is alive, never to die again, why would we think that Jesus wouldn't keep showing up in our midst even today?

In a few minutes, we'll come to the Lord's table and eat the bread and drink from the cup. The sacrament has been called "the Word acted out." The gospel proclaims the good news this Easter Sunday

— "Christ is risen! He is risen indeed!" Now we are invited to meet the risen Lord at his table. Easter is not, first and foremost, about agreeing intellectually with the correct or provable explanation about how the tomb could have been empty 2000 years ago. Easter is not, primarily, about begrudgingly giving in to some shaky propositions about life after death. But, then again, Easter is not about checking our minds at the sanctuary door and blindly accepting some ancient doctrine about a man who was crucified and said to have been raised up from the dead.

Easter is about meeting the risen Lord Jesus Christ, who keeps showing up in our midst, even when we hide out behind locked doors and four walls. Easter is about the risen Jesus showing up and standing in our midst — still today, 2000 years later — and giving us his peace and filling us with his Holy Spirit and sending us out from inside these four walls and from behind whatever doors we have locked because we are afraid. Easter is about meeting the risen, living Lord Jesus Christ — in the Word, in the water, in the bread, in the cup. Easter is about, even in the midst of the doubts that life forces upon us, finding ourselves saying with Thomas, "My Lord and my God!"

A friend and minister colleague recently told about two strangers showing up at the church unannounced and asking if they could pray in the sanctuary. The church secretary said, "Of course," and took them to the sanctuary. The maintenance man was vacuuming in the sanctuary, but he stopped to give the two people the space and quiet time they needed. He did watch what they did, however. The two visitors sat in each pew in the sanctuary and prayed for the people who sit there on Sunday. They stood in the pulpit and prayed for the minister. They sat in the choir loft and prayed for the choir members. They sang some hymns. When they were finished, they found the church secretary and thanked her and asked if they could pray with her. "Of course," she said. Then the two strangers went on their way.

Jesus keeps showing up! Jesus keeps showing us that although he was crucified, he is alive and with us still today. Jesus keeps saying, "Peace be with you." Jesus keeps giving us the power of the Holy Spirit. Jesus keeps sending us out from behind our locked doors and our fears. Jesus keeps calling us to trust in him.

Christ is risen! He is risen indeed!

And he keeps showing up . . .

Thanks be to God!

NOTES

[1]William H. Willimon, "A Visitation: Epiphany Meditation." Rev. David Bowman shared this article with me in Rocky Mount, NC in the early 1980's. I am unable to locate the proper citation for the magazine or journal in which it originally appeared.

The Dance of Love
Isaiah 6:1-8; Romans 8:12-17

The boys in Mrs. Davis' 7th grade class at Garden Hills Elementary School in Atlanta used to be dismayed when it rained. Rain meant we couldn't go outside and play kickball. Rain meant we had to stay inside and folk dance and square dance in the narrow, crowded hall. Actually, in 7th grade, I guess the guys had some mixed feelings about dancing with the girls. I just remember most of us wanting to be out on the playground playing kickball!

Although I never got to meet Nancy's father, she tells me he loved to dance, especially to beach music. Her mom and dad used to triple date with two other couples and go out dancing on a regular basis. And her parents were both raised Baptist! They did become Presbyterians, though, after they met in college and got married.

A prima ballerina may put on a virtuoso solo performance . . .

A budding ballet dancer may dance solo in front of the mirror . . .

But most of the time, dancing involves more than one person. Why else would we say, "It takes two to tango" or talk about dance companies or dance troupes?

There's something about dancing that is intimate and moving. Think about the traditional father-of-the-bride/bride dance and the mother-of-the-groom/groom dance at the reception. Think about gliding across the dance floor with that special person for the first time. Think about working as one with your dance partner as you make the spins and dips. In her song, "Alice and Roy," Carrie Newcomer sings about a husband and wife, both 90 years old, who spy a young couple in a diner. They start reminiscing about their own relationship, and she sings, "Back during the war at a wild country-dance, He thought she'd ignore him but he took the chance, Fifteen songs later he still held her close And a million dances since then hasn't been enough."

This morning I'd like for us to think about "the dance of love." On the church calendar, today is marked as Trinity Sunday. That should be pretty obvious based on the hymns we're singing, the Opening Sentences, the margin notes, and the benediction. Today is the only Sunday in the church calendar that is devoted to a doctrine of the church. Christmas is about the doctrine of the incarnation and we hear stories about the shepherds and the wise men and the baby in the manger. Good Friday is about the doctrine of the atonement and we hear stories about Jesus' death on the cross on Calvary. Easter is about the doctrine of the resurrection and we hear stories about an empty tomb and the risen Lord appearing to his disciples. Pentecost is about the doctrines of the church and the Holy Spirit and we hear stories about the Spirit coming upon the disciples "like the rush of a violent wind" with "divided tongues, as of fire" resting on the disciples. But you won't find any stories about the Trinity anywhere in the Bible. You won't find any particular verse that says something like, "The Trinity means . . ."

My goal today, as it is on every Trinity Sunday, is NOT to preach a sermon that *explains* the doctrine of the Trinity. I'm not even sure that it's possible or desirable to **explain** the doctrine of the Trinity. The desert father and intellectual Evagrios of Pontus from the 4th century spent the last sixteen years of his life in the Egyptian desert with Coptic Christians. He said, "God cannot be grasped by the mind. If he could be grasped he would not be God."[1]

As I said, my goal today is NOT to explain the doctrine of the Trinity, I'm convinced that the idea of the Trinity did not come about because some people long ago sat around and tried to think up a difficult theological idea for us to puzzle over 2000 years later. I think the idea of "God in three persons, blessed Trinity" occurred to God's people — became fundamental for God's people — because that is how they experienced God's amazing grace and love in their lives and in their history.

Maybe the closest we come to any kind of explicit statement of the Trinity in the New Testament is the benediction I use at the end of every worship service: "The grace of the Lord Jesus Christ, the love of God, and the communion of the Holy Spirit be with all of you." Thousands of books have been written about each of those three phrases — the grace of Jesus Christ, the love of God, the communion of the Holy Spirit — and the theological works are important for our faith. But it is the relationship that is expressed in and through that benediction that is at the core of our own faith and relationship with God, the Father, the Son, and the Holy Spirit. One of the early church fathers, Tertullian of the late 1st and early 2nd centuries A.D., wrote, "Who can know the truth without the help of God? Who can know God without Christ? Who has ever discovered Christ without the Holy Spirit?"[2]

For centuries, believes have used many different symbols to understand, explain, and communicate the meaning of the Trinity, God the three-in-one. There is St. Patrick's shamrock. There are three interlocking circles that look like a Venn diagram. There is the equilateral triangle. There is the fleur-de-lis. There is the example of water, ice, and steam, all the same but each different — or the sun, the sunbeams, and the warmth of the sun, all the same but each one different.

Today's bulletin has a different — maybe new to you — symbol of the Trinity in the upper lefthand corner on the front. Look at one artist's depiction of three dancing figures, and listen to one unknown writer's description of the Father, Son, and Spirit: "Father, Son, and Spirit. . . [are engaged in a] dance which is their life together, a dance without beginning and without end, a dance which is joy beyond all telling . . . The music of this eternal dance echoes in the vast reaches between the stars, and pulses in worlds inside of atoms, and travels on every breeze across the earth, and surges with the blood through our veins. From time to time, we hear the music of this eternal dance.

During the silences when everything makes sense; during the celebrations when we taste a bit of heaven . . . When we are thankful for what we've been given, proud of what we've done, hopeful about what the future holds. It is on these great and good occasions that we hear the music of the eternal dance, the rhythm of the Trinity. The Trinity is unending, joyous dance, yet the miracle is that the circle breaks open, and the Son and Spirit, still holding hands with the Father, extend their other hands to us, inviting us into the circle, drawing us into the dance, that we may become their partners, participants in their life."[3]

In his letter to the Romans, the apostle Paul doesn't talk about "the dance of love," but when he writes about "Life in the Spirit," he describes a beautifully choreographed relationship among God the Father, God the Son, and God the Spirit. As the writer puts it, "the Son and the Spirit, still holding hands with the Father, extend their other hands to us, inviting us into the circle, drawing us into the dance, that we may become their partners, participants in their life." Paul says, "For all who are led by the Spirit of God are children of God . . . you have received a spirit of adoption . . . it is that very Spirit bearing witness with our spirit that we are children of God, and if children, then heirs, heirs of God and joint heirs with Christ." (Romans 8:14-17)

Imagine that! Not only are we children of God, but we are heirs. We have been written into the will. We are in line for a full inheritance of all that God has promised. We've been invited to join the dance of love!

I remember when Nancy and I got the news from the adoption agencies that we had been matched with our children. We danced around the living room with joy! I remember when we got the final adoption decrees from the Halifax County courts and read the phrase, "Adopted for life." Those are wonderful metaphors for God the Three-in-One. Imagine God, Father, Son, and Holy Spirit dancing for joy when they are matched with us as their children! Imagine God the Three-in-One decreeing, "You are my children, adopted for life — not just never-ending life, but for life itself, for living, for love!"

Two contemporary Christian writers have used this early Christian idea of the divine dance of love to talk about our relationship with God, Father, Son, and Holy Spirit. Timothy Keller, pastor of the Redeemer Presbyterian Church in New York City, says that, in the Trinity, "Each of the divine persons centers upon the others. None demands that the others revolve around him. Each voluntarily circles the other two, pouring love, delight, and adoration into them. Each person of the Trinity loves, adores, defers to, and rejoices in the other. That creates a dynamic, pulsating dance of joy and love."[4]

Brian McLaren, a pastor, theologian, writer, and speaker, talks about how the early church leaders used the image of the "circle dance" to describe the Trinity. "The Trinity was an eternal dance of the Father, Son and Spirit sharing mutual love, honor, happiness, joy and respect . . . God's act of creation means that God is inviting more and more beings into the eternal dance of Joy. Sin means that people are stepping out of the dance.... stomping on feet instead of moving with grade, rhythm and reverence. Then in Jesus, God enters creation to restore the rhythm and beauty again."[5]

At the end of every LOGOS Wednesday, after the tables have been cleared and we have played our table game, we all hold hands in a big circle in the Fellowship Hall. We sing "Happy Birthday" and the Doxology or Gloria Patri. I don't think we've ever danced! Nevertheless, the circle unites us as one body. Sometimes the circle is broken, but it's only to let other folks join in. Two people, still holding hands with the others, extend their other hands to other people on the outside, inviting them into the circle, drawing them into the dance, that they may become their partners. We frequently remind one another that the only rule of LOGOS is "Everyone will treat everyone else as a child of God."

"It is that very Spirit bearing witness with our spirit that we are children of God, and if children, then heirs, heirs of God and joint heirs with Christ" — one God, Father, Son, and Holy Spirit.

Our closing hymn today is at the request of the Wednesday morning Bible study group, who said, "We **are** going to sing 'Lord of the Dance' on Sunday, right?" When Bible study was over, I e-mailed Cheryl and texted Vera and Karla and changed the order and selection of today's hymns. Hymn #157 is not particularly a Trinitarian hymn, but if we think about God the Son dancing with joy and love with God the Father and God the Spirit, how can we sit this one out?

Dance, then, wherever you may be;

I am the Lord of the Dance, said he,

and I'll lead you all, wherever you may be,

and I'll lead you all in the dance, said he.

NOTES

[1-5] All of the citations in this sermon are from "The Dance of Love: Perichoresis," at www.musicanddancing.wordpress.com/perichoresis/

Sacred Cows and Best Practices
Exodus 20:1-17; Mark 7:1-23

In response to a blog about "what matters and what doesn't" in the church, a minister remembered his first, rural, red-front-doors congregation. When the people gathered for worship, the members of the church council sat on the back row of the church every Sunday. The attendance of other members of the congregation varied, but each Sunday the council members lined up on the back row of the sanctuary. After he had been there a couple of months, the minister had to ask, "Why do you all sit lined up on the back row?"

It seems that, when the congregation was very young, the congregation was afraid of an Indian attack. The church council took on the job of watching from the bell tower for approaching danger. Although the church was never attacked, the council members did spot a house fire one time. After one hundred twenty-five years, the council members still sat lined up on the back row of the sanctuary.[1]

Someone has commented that we church folks are good "at making a trivial thing into a tradition, making the tradition into symbol, turning the symbol into faith, and finally transforming the symbol into law."[2] For instance, consider the white cloth that covers the communion table in many churches. My first memory of communion is from the Shades Valley Presbyterian Church in Birmingham, Alabama. The table was set with the bread and cup trays and everything was covered with a white cloth.

In some churches, the removal of the white tablecloth is an elaborate production, with the elders or women of the Church carefully folding the tablecloth, almost as if they were folding an American flag at a graveside service. But, do you know why some churches, especially in the South, started putting white tablecloths over the communion elements of bread and wine? Before there was air conditioning, churches would have the windows and doors open on a Sunday morning so the breeze could blow through. With the doors and windows open, flies would come in and land on the bread and cup. The white tablecloth kept the flies off the elements.

Once air conditioning was introduced in churches, the doors and windows were shut and the flies stayed outside. Still, many churches continued to cover their communion tables with white tablecloths. They even developed meaning and symbolism for the cloth, none of which can be found in the biblical accounts of Jesus eating the Last Supper with his disciples. As with so many things in the church, the original purpose of the practice was forgotten, but the tradition was strongly maintained.

When I was in seminary, I drove to New Orleans on a break to stay with my elderly grandfather for a few days. We called him Bumpa. On Sunday morning, we went to our family church where I was baptized and where my grandfather had served as an elder and clerk of session. Bumpa had told the minister that I was coming to visit and that I was a seminary student. The minister invited me to read one of the scripture lessons during worship that day. When it was time for the offering and offertory, the minister reached under the pulpit, pulled out a violin, and began to play the offertory. He was quite good, and apparently he played in worship quite often. However, my grandfather didn't think very highly of his minister playing the violin in the worship service. I have often wondered what Bumpa would think of me playing handbells in worship!

Another Presbyterian minister who played the violin ran into problems about music in worship. Here is an excerpt from a late 19th century book by Robert Alison called *The Anecdotage of Glasgow*. "The Rev. Dr. William Ritchie of St. Andrew's Church, Glasgow, was exceedingly fond of music, and had taught his church to admire both vocal and instrumental music combined. They determined, if possible, to secure an organ, to assist in aiding the praise in public worship, but were not allowed to do so by the Presbytery, which was of the 'opinion that the use of organs in the public worship of God is contrary to the law of the land and constitution of our Established Church.'

"This did not, however, prevent Dr. Ritchie cultivating his favorite art. He loved the violin especially, and had both a big and a small one, which he frequently used. Though popular with his own congregation, who were devoted to him, and admired his ministrations, he was not so well liked by his brethren, who thought he acted an unministerial part by playing on the violin. In the year 1807 he was waited upon by a deputation of ministers, to advise him to give up his performances of these instruments on a Saturday night, that he might be the better prepared in spirit for the sacred duties of the Sabbath day. When they arrived, Dr. Ritchie asked them to come in, and he would let them hear one of his favorite tunes, and then they could judge for themselves whether such music was calculated to produce evil or good results.

"They consented to remain, and he begged them not to interrupt him in the performance till he was done, which would be, at most, in a few minutes. Taking the largest instrument into his hands, he played with care and feeling his own most favorite tune, the *Old Hundred*. The effect was marked. One of the chief divines was entranced, and could not refrain from saying — 'Oh, 'tis a heavenly sound! please let us hear it again.'

"Dr. Ritchie, marking the favorable impression made, played several sacred pieces to the admiration of the deputation, some of whom declared themselves converts to the beneficial effect upon the mind of sweet sounds."[3]

In our gospel story this morning, the Pharisees complain to Jesus about his disciples, "Why don't your disciples live according to the tradition of the elders?" Jesus quotes from the prophet Isaiah ("This people honors me with their lips, but their heart is far away from me."). He then calls their beloved practices into question when he says, "Forsaking the commandment of God you hold fast to human tradition . . . You well set aside the commandment of God, in order that you might make stand your tradition. . . You cancel the word of God by your tradition." (Mark 7:8, 9, 13)

There are many discussions — even controversies and fights, what some call the "Worship Wars" — in churches these days. What style of worship will we offer? What kinds of instruments will we allow in the sanctuary? Who can use the church building and for what purposes? What traditions will we build on and what new things will we introduce? What traditions and symbols and ways of doing things have served their purpose and need to be retired? What traditions do we hold onto, even if we can't remember the reason why the practice was started in the first place?

Bishop Peter Storey served for many years as a South African Methodist minister and was very involved in the anti-apartheid struggle and its aftermath. For seven years, he taught at the Duke Divinity School in Durham. When he returned to South Africa, he helped design and build a Methodist seminary and served as interim president. This distinguished and faithful servant of the Lord, with forty years of ministry, has said, "It is easier to do church than to be church." That is so true — especially when it comes to traditions and customs and rituals and "the way we've always done it."

When Jesus criticized the Pharisees and certain of the scribes "who had come from Jerusalem," he didn't tell them not to obey and follow God's law. Instead, he criticized them for putting their own traditions and ways of doing things on a higher level than God's law, and then using God's law as a justification for what they wanted to do anyway. Jesus used a particular example based on the commandment "Honor your father and your mother." By designating as a gift for God what could have been used to help one's parent, Jesus said to the religious leaders, you actually go against the purpose of God's law about honoring your parents. And yet, you puff yourselves up and claim that your traditions take priority.

In his commentary on this gospel story, Lamar Williamson says, "By emphasizing the secondary place of human traditions and the primary place of the commandment of God, this text calls us beyond arguments over what is old and what is new to a concern for what is vital."[4] In that sense, Jesus is not condemning all traditions and rituals in the church, and neither should we. On the other hand, when we set *our* traditions, rites, and laws in stone and they end up getting in the way of our keeping God's law, then we have a problem. When our traditions and "the way we've always done things" become sacred cows and quit being the best practices for helping us do what vital in the church, then we have a problem.

Last Sunday, the members of the Alternative Sunday School Class had an interesting discussion about Chapter 10 of N.T. Wright's book, *small faith — GREAT GOD*. The chapter is called "Christian Hypocrites?" On a Monday morning years ago, our church secretary told me about the evangelist who had preached the night before at her church's revival. He said people often say to him, "I don't go to church because there are so many hypocrites there." So he asks them, "Do you go to WalMart? There are lots of hypocrites there!"

Nobody likes to be called a hypocrite, with its implication of being two-faced and insincere. And yet, that's what Jesus called the religious leaders and church people who let their traditions and ways of doing things get in the way of doing what God really called them to do and to be as his people. In his chapter, N.T. Wright says, "We tithe the mint and dill and cumin — we may be scrupulously careful about how we spend Sunday, we may never go to the theater, we may have a regular quiet time, which we never miss, we may know how to dot the i's and cross the t's of the finer points of doctrine — and then when it comes to the weightier matters of the law, we fall flat on our faces — justice and love."[5]

The word "hypocrite" originated from the stage and theater, and referred to the role an actor or actress played. In light of this gospel story, in which Jesus chastises the religious folk for being hypocrites, he seems to be saying, "Don't play-act to obey God's law." As someone has said, Jesus doesn't want us to be actors of the word, but doers of the word.

The story is told about Mark Twain attending a church service after the minister, who was a friend of Twain's, had repeatedly urged him to come. The minister worked very hard on his sermon during the week, in anticipation of preaching before the great Mark Twain. However, as he preached, he couldn't help but notice that Mark Twain seemed to be completely unmoved, even uninterested, in his sermon.

After the service, Mark Twain told the minister, "I have a book at home with every word you preached this morning." The minister was quite upset and assured Mark Twain that he had worked hard on the sermon that week, that it was original, and that he had never preached it before. Still, Mark Twain claimed to have a book with every word the minister had preached. "I want to see this book," demanded the minister.

The next day the minister found a neatly wrapped package from Twain at his front door. When he opened the package, he found a dictionary. Inside the front cover, Mark Twain had written, "Words, just words, just words."[6]

Our congregation will mark its 131st anniversary in November. We have a long history of faithful service to our Lord Jesus Christ and this community. We also have 131 years of traditions and ways of doing things. Let us hope and pray that our traditions will always help us remember and do what is most vital. Let us hope and pray and act to be the church and not just do church.

NOTES

[1] Janet H. Hunt, "Dancing with the Word" blog at www.words.dancingwiththeword.com/2012/08/what-matters-and-what-doesnt_25.html

[2] Found at www.forums.insearchoftruth.org

[3] Robert Alison, *The Anecdotage of Glasgow (1892)* found at www.electricscotland.com.

[4] Lamar Williamson, Jr., *Luke* (Atlanta: John Knox Press, 1983), p. 136.

[5] N.T. Wright, *small faith, GREAT GOD* (Downers Grove, IL: IVP Books, 2010), p. 95.

[6] Adapted from two different sources: Johan Cilliers, *The Living Voice of the Gospel: Revisiting the basic principles of preaching* (Stellenbosch, South Africa, 2004), p. 25 and Tim Snider, *All Things New: Understanding the Book of Revelation* (Bloomington, IN: 2011), p. 93.

My Whole Life Long
Romans 8:31-39; Psalm 71:1-24

When I get older, losing my hair,

Many years from now.

Will you still be sending me a valentine,

Birthday greetings, bottle of wine?

If I'd been out till quarter to three,

Would you lock the door?

Will you still need me, will you still feed me,

When I'm sixty-four?

That Beatles' song was the first song recorded for the 1967 album Sgt. Pepper's Lonely Hearts Club Band. The original plan was to release "When I'm 64" as the B-side to "Strawberry Fields Forever" or "Penny Lane." Eventually those two songs were released as a double A-side single and "When I'm 64" was included on Sgt. Pepper's.

Did you know that Paul McCartney wrote "When I'm 64" when he was 16 years old in 1958? When the Beatles were still known as The Quarrymen, they would sometimes play "When I'm 64" when their amps overheated after a long playlist. They would gather around a piano and sing this song. Some people think Paul McCartney was inspired to include the song on Sgt. Pepper's because his father, Jim McCartney, had turned sixty-four a few months before the album was recorded. [It's interesting to note that Sir Paul will be *74* in June!]

"When I get older, losing my hair, many years from now... Will you still need me, will you still feed me when I'm sixty-four?" In those bouncy lyrics in which a young man asks his girlfriend if she'll stick with him through the years, I heard echoes of the psalmist's cry to the Lord: "Do not cast me off in the time of old age; do not forsake me when my strength is spent... O God, from my youth you have taught me, and I still proclaim your wondrous deeds. So even to old age and gray hairs, O God, do not forsake me, until I proclaim your might to all the generations to come." (Psalm 71:9, 17-18)

If the psalmist were to channel Paul McCartney and ask the Lord, "Will you still need me, will you still feed me when I'm sixty-four?" he answers his own question throughout his psalm:

* For you are my rock and my fortress

* For you, O Lord, are my hope

* For you are my trust, O Lord, from my youth

* O God, from my youth you have taught me

* You will increase my honor and comfort me once again

* I will praise you for your faithfulness

* My lips will shout for joy when I sing praises to you; my soul also, which you have rescued.

Thursday morning I sat down in my study to write this sermon. I turned on Pandora Radio on my computer and put it on a station I had created called "Communion Song Radio." As I got ready to write the sermon, I bowed my head and prayed to God to help me as I worked. As I prayed, there was some music playing in the background, but I can't tell you what song was playing. However, as I repeated that simple prayer two or three times, all of a sudden I realized the words to the song on Pandora were crystal clear. Here is the song by Steven Curtis Chapman that was playing:

As I look back on the road I've traveled,
I see so many times He carried me through;
And if there's one thing that I've learned in my life,
My Redeemer is faithful and true.
My Redeemer is faithful and true.

My Redeemer is faithful and true.
Everything He has said He will do,
And every morning His mercies are new.

Philip Gladden

My Redeemer is faithful and true.

My heart rejoices when I read the promise
'There is a place I am preparing for you.'
I know someday I'll see my Lord face to face,
'Cause my Redeemer is faithful and true.
My Redeemer is faithful and true.

And in every situation He has proved His love to me;
When I lack the understanding, He gives more grace to me.

I picked our final hymn to serve as something of an answer to the psalmist's plea to the Lord, "Do not cast me off in the time of old age; do not forsake me when my strength is spent . . . So even to old age and gray hairs, O God, do not forsake me."

"I Was There to Hear Your Borning Cry" has been described as "a love song to humanity" which "gives us a sense of the timelessness of God . . . The spirit of 'Borning Cry' is one of a God who loved us from the beginning of time and continues to love us throughout the seasons of our life."[1] The song was written to accompany a video series about baptism in the Lutheran Church. The note at the bottom of Hymn #488 in our hymnbook says, "this hymn speaks in the imagined conversational voice of God, assuring the person being baptized of God's presence throughout the changing stages of life."

I was there to hear your borning cry;
I'll be there when you are old.
I rejoiced the day you were baptized to see your life unfold.
I was there when you were but a child
with a faith to suit you well;
in a blaze of light you wandered off to find where demons dwell.

When you heard the wonder of the Word,
I was there to cheer you on.
You were raised to praise the living Lord to whom you now belong.
If you find someone to share your time and you join your hearts as one,
I'll be there to make your verses rhyme from dusk to rising sun.

In the middle ages of your life, not too old, no longer young,
I'll be there to guide you through the night, complete what I've begun.
When the evening gently closes in and you shut your weary eyes,
I'll be there as I have always been with just one more surprise.
I was there to hear your borning cry;
I'll be there when you are old.
I rejoiced the day you were baptized to see your life unfold.

On Tuesday, I sat down with my Bible and a blank legal pad. I decided to do a slow reading of Psalm 71 and jot down the words and phrases that spoke to me. I didn't really intend to outline the psalm, but that's what I ended up doing, in a sense. As I looked back over what I had written down, I noticed two things.

First, the psalmist is very honest in his talk with God. There is absolutely no sense that just because he believes in and trusts in God, he is somehow spared the problems of life. He prays,

* Be to me a rock of refuge, a strong fortress to save me.

* In your righteousness deliver me and rescue me; incline your ear to me and save me.

* Rescue me, O my God, from the hand of the wicked, from the grasp of the unjust and cruel.

* My enemies speak concerning me, [because they think you have forsaken me].

* Let my accusers be put to shame . . . let those who seek to hurt me be covered with scorn and disgrace.

* You who have made me see many troubles and calamities will revive me again; from the depths of the earth you will bring me up again.

Second, again and again the psalmist returns to praise the Lord.

* My praise is continually for you.

* My mouth is filled with your praise, and with your glory all day long.

* But I will hope continually, and will praise you yet more and more.

* I will come praising the mighty deeds of the Lord God, I will praise your righteousness, yours alone.

* I will also praise you with the harp for your faithfulness, O God; I will sing praises to you with the lyre, O Holy One of Israel.

* My lips will shout for joy when I sing praises to you.

* All day long my tongue will talk of your righteous help.

The framework of the psalm is Praise to the Lord. That framework of praise and trust is what sees the psalmist through the long-haul of life. And we all know that in the long-haul of life, we will cry out to God many times, "Rescue me, O my God, save me, do not be far from me, help me!" No matter how old you are, you may find yourself crying to God, "Do not cast me off, do not forsake me."

Each time the psalmist asks the Lord for help, the psalmist also makes a sturdy statement of hope and trust in what the Lord has done and can do. As someone has said, "Praise becomes an ongoing, continual action of living a sacrificial life of worship. Whatever we do in word, action, thought, or deed is to reflect the goodness of the God in whom we place our hope and trust."

There is a story about William Preston Few, the first president of Duke University, who oversaw the school's transition from Trinity College. President Few was walking to church one Sunday in the pouring rain. A group of students passed by him in a car, recognized who he was, and offered him a ride, which he accepted. When President Few got in the car, the students asked him why he had decided to go to church on such a miserable day. He replied, "I did not decide to go to church THIS MORNING. I decided more than fifty years ago, and I have not had to ask myself the question since then." It was a regular part of his life. It was what he did.[2]

That story about President Few walking through the rain to praise the Lord seems to be a good parable about trusting and praising the Lord my whole life long. There will be miserable, rainy days in our lives — literally and figuratively. When you get soaked to the skin, when you feel like you're going under for the third time, when you cry out to God, "Rescue me!" you can remember that God has always been there for you — from your borning cry — and that God has promised to be there for you always — whether you're 4 or 64 or 94!

Sometimes older folks say to me, "I wonder why I'm still here. What purpose do I have?" That is a heartfelt question, the same question the psalmist seems to be asking. But that question doesn't come just from gray headed people looking back over their long lives. Every stage of life has its challenges. At any stage along the way, you can feel like your strength is spent. You might wonder "What purpose do I have?"

One thing you can say about the psalms — they are quite honest and open about the way life is. Our psalm today deals with that very question — "What purpose do I have?" — and the fear that comes along with it, the fear that somehow God has forgotten about us. But the psalmist is like President Few walking to church through the rain. He decided long ago to hope and trust in the Lord — not because his life never has any challenges or rain, but because he knows he can depend on the Lord even when life is soaking him through to the skin.

Here's a version of Psalm 71 written by Silvia Purdie. As I read it, listen for the alternating voices, old and young, in each line. It begins with an older person.

All my life long you have been with me.
When I was born and took my first breath, you held me.
All through the years I have leaned on you.
Through all the years ahead I will lean on you.
When I was young you taught me.

When I grow old you will bless me.
I remember all you have done for me.
I will tell everyone how great you are!
It hasn't always been easy. People have attacked me.
It isn't always easy. Some problems seem really big.
But I hope continually. I trust and keep on trusting.
I sing and keep on singing.
My lips will shout for joy, my soul also, for you have rescued me.
I will play the guitar and the drums, to praise you loudly!
I will put your love into words for anyone who will listen.
Your power and glory reaches from high above to deep below.
Your saving grace reaches from before we were born to our very last breath, and beyond.
Holy One, wonderful God, we praise you!
Holy One, marvelous Lord, we praise you!

NOTES

[1] C. Michael Hawn, "History of Hymns: 'I Was There to Hear Your Borning Cry,'" Discipleship Ministries, The United Methodist Church at www.umcdiscipleship.org.

[2] This illustration is taken from a sermon by Rev. Alex Evans, Second Presbyterian Church, Richmond, VA, "Reckless, Faithful, Cheerful Generosity," October 25, 2015.

God's Future for The Here and Now
Galatians 3:23-29; Revelation 7:1-17

The odds of you winning the $1.5 billion Powerball lottery jackpot in January were 1 in 292.2 million or .000000003422.

The odds of you being struck by lightning in a given year (based on reported injuries and deaths) are 1 in 1,190,000 or .0000008403.

The odds of you being attacked by a shark are 1 in 3,748,067 or .0000002668.

The odds of you going to heaven depend on whether you are talking about all people who have ever lived or just all Christians who have ever lived. In the case of all human beings who have ever lived, your odds are 144,000 in 108 billion or .000001333. If you calculate the odds in terms of all Christians, your odds are 144,000 in 13.5 billion or .00001066.

If you invest the $2 cost of the Powerball ticket for 20 years at 6% interest, you'll earn $4.40 interest, for a total of $6.40, which is still a better return than odds of .000000003422.

As long as you use common sense and try to be safe, you might as well swim in the ocean or go about your daily business even when the weather is stormy. Chances are good you won't get attacked by a shark or struck by lightning.

But what about going to heaven? The minuscule odds are based on the number 144,000 in Revelation 7:4 and estimates of the total number of people who have lived in history and the total number of Christians who have lived since the first century A.D.

Actually, the odds of you going to heaven are really 0% — IF you go by the teachings of the Jehovah's Witnesses. The full number of 144,000 believers who go to heaven was calculated beginning with Pentecost in 33 A.D. and ending in 1935, when the full number was reached. Of course, you had to be a Jehovah's Witness in the first place to have any chance of being counted among the 144,000.

Philip Gladden

I say all of that with my tongue somewhat firmly planted in my cheek, but also for serious, theological reasons. How you understand and interpret the book of Revelation makes all the difference in the world. Obviously, you can interpret John's writing literally, which will lead you to conclude that only 144,000 believers go to heaven (interestingly and conveniently, people from your own group).

Or, you can read and interpret Revelation as a message written to give God's people hope and assurance "for the living of these days," whether those days were in the latter part of the first century A.D. or in April 2016.

Not to belabor the number 144,000, but Revelation is full of symbolism and numerology. How do you get 144,000? 12 x 12 = 144. 12 tribes of Israel x 12 apostles = 144 x 1,000 (which in the Greek language/numerical system was a GREAT number). So 144,000 is a great, symbolic number — perhaps suggesting vastness and completeness.

But the 144,000 pales in comparison to what we read in Revelation 7:9: "After this I looked, and there was a great multitude that no one could count, from every nation, from all tribes and peoples and languages, standing before the throne and before the Lamb, robed in white, with palm branches in their hands. They cried out in a loud voice, saying, 'Salvation belongs to our God who is seated on the throne, and to the Lamb!'"

When John received his revelation from the Lord on the island of Patmos, he "was in the spirit on the Lord's day." (Rev. 1:10) We take this to mean he was worshiping on the first day of the week, on Sunday. Throughout Revelation, John gives us glimpses of the worship going on in heaven (particularly in Revelation 4 & 5) while he is worshiping on Patmos.

Think about that! As we gather here this morning to worship God with our hymns and psalms and prayers and anthems and offerings and commitments, God is being worshiped by a great multitude that no one could count, from every nation, from all tribes and peoples and languages. Did you read the margin note next to the Opening Sentences, from N.T. Wright, who is a noted New Testament scholar and the former bishop of Durham in the Church of England? "That is what worship is all about. It is the glad shout of praise that arises to God the creator and God the rescuer from the creation that recognizes its maker, the creation that acknowledges the triumph of Jesus the Lamb. That is the worship that is going on in heaven, in God's dimension, all the time. **The question we ought to be asking is how best we might join in.**"

Many people read Revelation as a "road map of the future." They understand Revelation to be all about future events and the end times. Certainly there is a lot of "future tense" language in Revelation, but that future orientation was meant to help early Christians in the here and now as they tried to live faithful lives in the midst of trying times. The vision of "the way it will be" gave them assurance that the God they worshiped and served through Jesus Christ was trustworthy and able to follow through on his promises, not just in some far-away time and place, but right smack dab in the midst of their day-to-day struggles as Christians.

I've often said that I think corporate worship is one of the most important things — if not *the* most important thing we do as the Wallace Presbyterian Church. First, that's why we were created — "to glorify God and to enjoy him forever." Second, corporate worship reminds us (or should) that this Christian life isn't just about "me and Jesus." It's not just about "getting myself to heaven." Corporate worship reminds us that we are part of the body of Christ. Worship reminds us that even though God promises to know us each by name, God's purposes are much bigger than our own, individual lives. God doesn't need our worship, but we need to worship God. Finally, corporate worship reminds us of our calling as God's people. It can't be a coincidence that the word used for "worship" can also mean "serve." We are not here this morning to entertain or to be entertained, but to worship and serve our holy God, both in this sanctuary and beyond.

Let's go back to the future for a minute. Revelation does give us a vision of the future, but it's God's future that makes a difference in and determines our present. In a reflection on these verses which he called "Not Just About the Future," Eric Barreto writes, "Revelation is about God in the end. Revelation points us to a holy God who keeps promises, a God who ensures justice for the downtrodden and judgment against their oppressors. Revelation is about a God who creates the world and then sets it right again. Revelation is not about the destruction of the world but the way God will set it right again. In short, this book is not about us or what the future will hold as much as it is about a God in whom we can trust on our worst days as much as we can on our best days. . . Revelation is a book about today. Revelation is about the here and now. Revelation is about us, all of us, in this way. Here's why. When we imagine a world so transformed by God that an innumerable crowd of different people from different places speaking different languages gather together as one, we ought to be inspired to action, especially when that vision is so discordant with what we see in our everyday lives. But we ought to be moved not to will ourselves to become better people but to trust that God is already drawing us together, that God's promises are already made true even in a world that has stopped making sense. On the ground of God's promises, we cannot help but act and hope for something better."[1]

If Revelation 7 gives us a glimpse of God's future that can and does shape our here and now, the verses which Lydia read from Paul's letter to the Galatians hold out that very vision for our life together as the body of Christ right now: "for in Christ Jesus you are all children of God through faith. As many of you as were baptized into Christ have clothed yourselves with Christ. There is no longer Jew or Greek, there is no longer slave or free, there is no longer male and female; for all of you are one in Christ Jesus. And if you belong to Christ, then you are Abraham's offspring, heirs according to the promise." (Galatians 3:26-29)

As a worship leader on a weekly basis, sometimes it's hard to worship 100% on a Sunday morning. I find myself thinking about what's coming next in the order of service, thinking about who is in worship and who isn't and why, thinking about not dropping the communion plates of bread and trays of juice cups, thinking about what the children might ask me in the Children's Sermon, etc., etc.

So, as much as I love worshiping with all of you week in and week out, I also relish the times when I sit in the pew and worship. This happens most often at presbytery meetings. I sit in the congregation and lend my voice to the chorus of praise to God. I hear someone preach from the Word of God. I get to bow my head as someone else prays with and for me and the Church.

And I get to come to the table as a pilgrim and not as an administrator of the sacrament. In presbytery worship, we typically receive the bread and cup by going forward to tear a piece of bread and dip it in the cup. Because I like to sit near the front of the sanctuary, I get to watch my brothers and sisters come down the aisle to receive the sacrament. There we are — not a great multitude that no one could count but, nevertheless, God's people: young and old; black, white, Latino; ministers and elders; people standing straight and tall, people bent over; people holding out their hands in anticipation of receiving God's grace. As I watch the people of God coming forward, I catch a glimpse of the great multitude standing before the throne and before the Lamb, singing, "Blessing and glory and wisdom and thanksgiving and honor and power and might be to our God forever and ever!" Then we all return to our seats and get on with the business of being the Church, the people of God. As we worship, we serve. As we serve, we worship. Then we leave our meeting place and return to our different congregations throughout southeastern North Carolina, having been reminded of the power and grace and mercy of our God who sits on the throne and who calls us his children.

There is great value and comfort in catching a glimpse of God's future through John's eyes in Revelation. But there is also a great value and comfort and calling for the here and now. The great multitude that no one could count standing before God's throne and lifting their voices in praise inspires us to live into God's future today as we worship and serve.

Let it be, Lord. Let it be.

NOTES

[1] Eric Barreto, "Not Just About the Future," for April 17, 2016 at www.onscripture.com.

Words to Live by in Times Such as These

The Goal of Love
Leviticus 19:11-18; Romans 12:14-21; Matthew 5:43-48

The minister was preaching a sermon based on Jesus' command to love your enemies. She said, "Now, I'll bet that many of us feel as if we have enemies in our lives. So, raise your hand if you have many enemies." Quite a few people raised their hands. "Now," she said, "raise your hand if you have only a few enemies." Only about half as many people raised their hands. "OK," the minister said, "raise your hand if you have only one or two enemies." Even fewer people raised their hands. "See," she said, "most of us feel like we have enemies."

Then the minister said, "Now raise your hand if you have no enemies at all." She looked around and didn't see any hands raised. Just as the minister was about to continue with her sermon, she spotted a very, very old man sitting on the back row with his hand raised. With great difficulty, the old man stood up and proclaimed, "I have no enemies."

The minister was delighted and invited the old man to the front of the church. When the usher had helped the man make his way down the aisle, the minister took his hand in hers and said, "What a blessing! How old are you?" The old man said, "I'm 98 years old and I have no enemies." The minister said, "What a wonderful Christian life you lead! Tell us all how it is that you have no enemies." The old man looked the minister in the eye and said, "All of 'em have died!"

I figured a little humor wouldn't hurt as we think this morning about Jesus' words, "Love your enemies, and pray for those who persecute you" and the command from Leviticus, "you shall love your neighbor as yourself" and the apostle Paul's description of the Christian life, "Bless those who persecute you; bless and do not curse them."

In this extraordinary season, we are daily being bombarded with news about our "enemies" such as ISIS and terrorists. In the middle of this political season, the rhetoric from both sides is heated and, in some cases, the other side is painted as "the enemy." Some people say our country has never been so divided.

And yet, consider this: Five weeks before the Battle of Fort Sumter in April 1861, Abraham Lincoln was inaugurated to his first term as president. On Monday, March 4, 1861, he delivered his first inaugural address with the clouds of secession on the horizon. In his one-sentence second paragraph, Lincoln said, "I do not consider it necessary at present for me to discuss those matters of administration about which there is no special anxiety or excitement." The rest of his address dealt with the issues about which there **was** special anxiety and excitement — the question of slavery and the possibility of civil war.

After Lincoln had outlined in great detail his position on and approach to these pressing issues, he concluded with these remarks: "In *your* hands, my dissatisfied fellow-countrymen, and not in *mine*, is the momentous issue of civil war. The Government will not assail *you*. You can have no conflict without being yourselves the aggressors. *You* have no oath registered in heaven to destroy the Government, while I shall have the most solemn one to 'preserve, protect, and defend it.' I am loath to close. We are not enemies, but friends. We must not be enemies. Though passion may have strained it must not break our bonds of affection. The mystic chords of memory, stretching from every battlefield and patriot grave to every living heart and hearthstone all over this broad land, will yet swell the chorus of the Union, when again touched, as surely they will be, by the better angels of our nature."[1]

Well, most of the time we're not angels. And we're certainly not Abraham Lincoln! So what are we supposed to do with Jesus' hard command, "You have heard that it was said, 'You shall love your neighbor and hate your enemy.' But I say to you, Love your enemies and pray for those who persecute you"? In fact, what are we supposed to do with most of what Jesus tells us to do in his Sermon on the Mount? Turn the other cheek. Do not be angry with your brother or sister. Do not resist an evildoer. And, as if those commands weren't hard enough, Jesus wraps up this section of his sermon by telling us, "Be perfect, therefore, as your heavenly Father is perfect."

One interpretation is that Jesus knew exactly what he was telling us. He knew we could never meet these requirements and act in this way. So, the commands he gives in his Sermon on the Mount were intended to highlight our sins and shortcomings and our need for God's saving grace in Jesus Christ. Well, it's certainly true that we all are sinners and fall short of God's glory. And it's just as true that we all need God's saving grace in Jesus Christ. But what if Jesus really meant what he said?

Many folks have asked this past week, "Have you been watching the Olympics?" Yes, and haven't the athletes been amazing? Simone Biles lived up to and perhaps exceeded the expectations of her in gymnastics. I don't know about you, but I've never been able to figure out the scoring system in Olympics gymnastics. However, you probably have noticed that no-one ever receives a perfect "10" any more. The scoring system was changed a while back and now it's impossible to get that score.

But forty years ago at the Summer Olympics in Montreal, Nadia Comaneci stunned and[1] excited the world when she was awarded the first perfect "10" for her routine on the uneven bars. The manufacturer of the Olympics scoreboard, Omega SA, asked the Olympic organizers if the board needed to display four digits for gymnastics scores. The organizers told the company three digits were enough, because a perfect 10 was impossible. When Nadia was awarded the first ever perfect "10," the scoreboard read "1.00" and the crowd didn't realize at first what had happened. She went on to receive six additional perfect 10's and won gold medals in the all-around, the balance beam, the uneven bars, and bronze medal for the floor exercise.[2]

It seems as if being "perfect as our heavenly Father is perfect" is as impossible as a perfect 10 in gymnastics was thought to be. But that's hearing "perfect" as having arrived, as meeting some kind of moral or legal checklist. Actually, "perfect" here has more of the sense of working toward a goal or purpose. The Apostle Paul talks about this very thing in his letter to the Philippian Christians when he writes "that I may gain Christ and be found in him, not having a righteousness of my own that comes from the law, but one that comes through faith in Christ, the righteousness from God based on faith . . . Not that I have already obtained this or have already reached the goal; but I press on to make it my own, because Christ Jesus has made me his own." (Philippians 3:8-9, 12)

In my Bible, the verses from Romans 12 are under the headings, "The New Life in Christ" and "Marks of the True Christian." Someone has said, "Our only hope for loving our enemy is to be a new creation in Christ. And our only hope for being a new creation in Christ is to be reconciled to God through the death of his Son." That's the theological foundation for Jesus' commands about how to live as his followers and citizens of the kingdom of God.

The New Revised Standard Version of the Bible, which is what you have in the pew Bibles, translates Matthew 5:44-45 this way: "But I say to you, Love your enemies and pray for those who persecute you, so that you may be children of your Father in heaven." A couple of different translations help us better understand what it means to "be perfect as our heavenly Father is perfect." *The Message* translation puts it this way: "When someone gives you a hard time, respond with the energies of prayer, for then you are working out of your true selves, your God-created selves." The New Living Translation really gets at what is at stake with following Jesus' commands about how to live: "But I say to you, love your enemies! Pray for those who persecute you! In that way, you will be acting as true children of your Father in heaven."

When I was in Zambia in June 2013, I got to know a man from South Africa named Yuri. He had retired from teaching at the Justo Mwale Theological University after many years. He was a guest lecturer during the time I was on campus. We ate together on several occasions and had many lengthy conversations about the political situations in the U.S. and South Africa. In June 2013, Nelson Mandela was very ill and many people thought he might die at that time (he did die in December of that year). I asked Yuri what he thought would happen in his home country when Mandela died. Yuri said there were different opinions. One group was warning the white people to arm themselves against black violence and revenge. Yuri said cooler heads suggested that Mandela's legacy had prepared the country to move forward after his death.

On February 11, 1990, Nelson Mandela was released after spending twenty-seven years in prison. In 1994 he was elected president of South Africa. In the four years between his release and his election, there was much violence and many deaths in the country. There were predictions of a great bloodbath when he became president. Many people were convinced President Mandela would seek revenge on the white population. Instead, Mandela surprised his country and the world (and received much criticism from some of his own backers) when he not only called for peaceful relations between blacks and whites, but actually did what he was asking his people to do. He appointed Bishop Desmond Tutu to head up the Truth and Reconciliation Commission to deal with the atrocities committed during apartheid. He invited his former prison guard to be a guest of honor at his presidential inauguration ceremony. He invited the state prosecutor who had demanded the death penalty for Mandela at his trial in 1963 to enjoy a kosher meal with him. In 1995, he wore the green jersey of the national rugby team at the World Cup Final. During the years of apartheid, there was an international boycott against the South African rugby team and the Springbok jersey became a hated symbol. When the team won the championship, President Mandela presented the trophy to the team captain and said it was time to put aside hatred and enmity and become a united nation. On the twentieth anniversary of his release from prison, Mandela invited his former prison guard to join him for dinner.

Former President Bill Clinton recalled a conversation with Nelson Mandela in which he asked him, "Didn't you really hate them for what they did?" Mandela replied, "Oh, yeah, I hated them for a long time. I broke rocks every day in prison, and I stayed alive on hate. They took a lot away from me. They took me away from my wife, and it subsequently destroyed my marriage. They took me away from seeing my children grow up. They abused me mentally and physically. And one day, I realized they could take it all except my mind and my heart. Those things I would have to give to them, and I simply decided not to give them away." President Clinton asked President Mandela," What about when you were getting out of prison? As you walked down that dirt road to freedom, didn't you hate them then?" Mandela said, "As I felt the anger rising up, I thought to myself, 'They have already had you for twenty-seven years. And if you keep hating them, they'll have you again.' And I said, 'I want to be free.' And so I let it go. I let it go. As I walked out the door toward the gate that would lead to my freedom, I knew if I didn't leave my bitterness and hatred behind, I'd still be in prison."[3]

I have no easy answers this morning about fulfilling Jesus' command to love our enemies and pray for those who persecute us. The "LOVE" Jesus is talking about is not the warm fuzzy feeling you get when you're with someone special. The "LOVE" Jesus is talking about is a verb — love in action, love that seeks the best for the other person. When you couple *that* kind of love with our Lord's command to "be perfect," that is, to work toward the goal of living as God's beloved children *because of* the love God himself has already shown us in Jesus Christ, then we hear Jesus' call to be who we are — God's beloved children who are called to reflect and show and share God's love, not only in what we say but also in what we do and how we treat other people — and not just the people who will love us back.

If you find today's scripture lessons to be quite challenging, join the club! But listening to and taking seriously and living out Jesus' command to LOVE can help us resist the siren song of hate and vengeance that saturates our society. Is it easy? No! Is it dangerous? Could be! Does it run counter to the way the world operates? You bet! Can we be "perfect" in our love in terms of always getting it right? You know we can't! Is LOVE the proper response to God's mercies in our lives? Absolutely!

In the first letter bearing his name, John writes, "See what love the Father has given us, that we should be called children of God; and that is what we are. . . Beloved, let us love one another, because love is from God. . . We love because God first loved us. Those who say, 'I love God,' and hate their brothers or sisters, are liars; for those who do not love a brother or sister whom they have seen, cannot love God whom they have not seen. The commandment we have from him is this: those who love God must love their brothers and sisters also." (1 John 3:1; 4:7, 19-21)

In his commentary on the letter to the Galatians, St. Jerome, a 4th/5th century theologian and church father, told an old story about John the Evangelist. When John became very old, each week his disciples would carry him into the meeting place where the congregation had gathered to worship. Each week, the weak and feeble John would say, "Little children, love one another." After a number of weeks, perhaps wondering why the old man always said the same thing every week, they asked him, "Master, why do you always say this?" John replied, "Because it is the Lord's command, and if this only is done, it is enough."[4]

In a few minutes, we're going to sing "They'll Know We Are Christians by Our Love." This is a way to remember that when we act in LOVE, "then [we] are working out of our true selves, our God-created selves and "In that way, you [are] acting as true children of your Father in heaven." But our Lord Jesus reminds us that his LOVE is not just for those who love us back.

Yes, that's a hard command to hear and even harder to do. Someone said this week, "Maybe we just need to start with the small things in our lives." My response was, "Yes, because even the small things can become great things if we really live this way." The goal is LOVE. Let us pray.

NOTES

[1] Abraham Lincoln, "First Inaugural Address, Monday, March 4, 1861," at www.bartleby.com.

[2] "Nadia Comăneci," at www.en.wikipedia.org/wiki/Nadia Comăneci."

[3] Philip Yancey, "Happy Birthday, Nelson Mandela," July 19, 2013 at www.philipyancey.com. The final sentence in the quotation is taken from "Clinton on Mandela: Old story, new context?" Sunday, July 6, 2008, at www.xpostfactoid.blogspot.com.

[4] Ralph F. Wilson, "Stories about John from the Church Fathers: Love One Another," at www.jesuswalk.com.

Home for Christmas
Matthew 11:2-6; Isaiah 35:1-10

Here are the top seven sites that showed up after a Google search of the phrase "going home for Christmas."

* Going Home for the Holidays: 21 Questions You'll Be Asked When You Go Home for the Holidays

* Are you worried about going home for the holidays after Trump's win?

* Top 10 Ways to Survive Going Home for the Holidays

* Is There Anything Stranger than Going Home for the Holidays?

* Going Home for the Holidays — from the University of Massachusetts at Dartmouth (advice to freshmen going home for the first time since starting college)

* Not going home for the holidays? I *Won't* Be Home for Christmas — A defense of staying away during the holidays

* We Slacked About Going Home for the Holidays — Weird Parental Ticks [sic], Room Snooping, WiFi Passwords

Kind of makes you think twice about going home for Christmas, doesn't it? Or about the people who might be coming to your house!

When I was checking the news on my iPad Thursday morning and thinking about writing my sermon, I saw an article on FaceBook called "12 Secular Christmas Songs that are Actually About Advent." The sub-title was "Your no-guilt Advent playlist!" That headline got my attention, so I checked out the playlist: It's Beginning to Look a Lot Like Christmas; Silver Bells; Santa Claus is Coming to Town; All I Want for Christmas is My Two Front Teeth; All I Want for Christmas is You; Last Christmas; White Christmas; Frosty the Snowman; We Need a Little Christmas; Rudolph the Red-Nosed

Reindeer; and It's the Most Wonderful Time of the Year. The article's author writes, "a number of the secular (not even about the birth of Jesus) songs called 'Christmas' music should be classified as winter themed music or even Advent music. If you look at the lyrics of many popular Christmas songs, you will discover that they are actually about getting ready for and waiting for Christmas."[1]

If you were keeping count of the songs, you noticed I only named eleven. #12 was "I'll Be Home for Christmas." Earlier in the week, I had already spent some time reading about the history of that familiar Christmas song as I worked on this sermon, so it was particularly interesting to see it listed in a list of secular Christmas songs about Advent. "I'll be home for Christmas, you can plan on me, please have snow and mistletoe, and presents 'neath the tree." The article says, "There are a number of Christmas songs about wishing for a place or a person, and these are all symbolic of our Advent longing for Jesus to come as a little baby and to come again."

On October 4, 1943, Bing Crosby recorded "I'll Be Home for Christmas," which quickly became popular among U.S. troops overseas during World War II. It was the most requested song at USO shows. The lyricist, Kim Gannon, more than once said that he didn't write the song with soldiers in mind, but that he was "thinking of all people who are unable to be home for Christmas." At first, Gannon's song was rejected by the music business because the last line was thought to be too sad: "I'll be home for Christmas, if only in my dreams." However, Gannon sang the song for Bing Crosby as they were playing golf, and the rest is history.

The much-beloved Christmas song is very melancholy, and the last line is rather haunting: "if only in my dreams. . ." As one writer has put it, "While the melody is one that lingers in our minds, the meaning of the song is actually quite somber as the closing line reveals that being home for Christmas isn't quite a reality just yet."[2]

It might seem odd to you to hear about a melancholy secular song of longing on this third Sunday of Advent when we light the candle of JOY. And yet, that comment, "being home for Christmas isn't quite a reality just yet," expresses very well the tension of these weeks of Advent leading up to Christmas, as well as the challenge of living faithful Christian lives in this "time between the times," the already but not yet of God's restoration of his creation and his people when Christ returns at his second Advent.

The prophet Isaiah didn't preach and write his words for the third Sunday of Advent, but they are often used on this third Sunday of Advent, exactly because they ring out with the joy of going home — and not only going home, but being led home by God himself along God's highway through the wilderness. Isaiah proclaimed the promise of going home to God's people who had been away from home for fifty years, languishing in exile in Babylon. Their temple had been destroyed. Their capital city had been laid waste. Their citizens had been carted off to a foreign land and ridiculed. How could they possibly have hope in such a situation? How could they sing the Lord's song in a foreign land?

Sunday night, David Sanderson led off the community sing of "Messiah" with maybe his strongest rendition yet of "Comfort Ye My People." As David's voice reached a crescendo and filled the sanctuary of First Baptist Church, he sang, "Make straight in the desert a highway for our God." In other words, God is coming — get ready! This is a word of hope for God's people — then and now — and sets the tone for the rest of "Messiah."

That song is based on Isaiah 40:3, but it sounds a lot like Isaiah 35:8 and 10: "A highway shall be there, and it shall be called the Holy Way; the unclean shall not travel on it, but it shall be for God's people; no traveler, not even fools, shall go astray. And the ransomed of the Lord shall return, and come to Zion with singing; everlasting joy shall be upon their heads; they shall obtain joy and gladness, and sorrow and sighing shall flee away."

The pictures are powerful — the wilderness and the dry land; the desert; the burning sand and the thirsty ground. The wilderness calls to mind God's people wandering in the wilderness for forty years before they made it home to the Promised Land. But it wasn't aimless wandering, nor were they on their own. God was with them all along the way, a cloud by day, a pillar of fire by night, showing them the way to go home.

The wilderness calls to mind God's people languishing in exile for fifty years in Babylon, certainly reason for sorrow and sighing. But the prophet's message is one of hope and promise — "Courage! Take heart! God is here, right here, on his way to put things right and redress all wrongs. He's on his way! He'll save you!"

The wilderness calls to mind the times in our lives when we feel dried up spiritually, when we feel lost, when we can't find our way home. Maybe that's how you feel this morning, even in the midst of all of the holiday hoopla and busyness. Maybe "going home for Christmas" is fraught with anxiety for you, even if you're staying right here in Wallace. Maybe the way the world is today seems to be nothing more than a huge expanse of dry, dusty, barren desert. Where is the hope of the crocus and rose blossoms? Where is the promise of the lush greenery of Carmel and Sharon? Isaiah's message of hope and promise and, yes, even joy comes to us again this Advent —"Courage! Take heart! God is here, right here, on his way to put things right and redress all wrongs. He's on his way! He'll save you!" It's not a joy that depends on whether or not all of the decorations are put up just right or if all of the Christmas shopping is done on time or the house is just right for the family and friends who are coming home. Instead, the joy of this third Sunday of Advent is rooted in the prophet's proclamation, "They shall see the glory of the Lord, the majesty of our God."

Two months after Bing Crosby recorded "I'll Be Home for Christmas," the crew of the battleship U.S.S. North Carolina was in the Pacific Ocean near the New Hebrides Islands on Christmas Eve 1943. The crew had been ordered to ship out on Christmas morning to provide support for a carrier attack.

The crew gathered on Christmas Eve for an entertaining show with skits, dances, comedy routines, a fake strip tease, and a drag show with guys wearing wigs made out of manila rope. Can you imagine the melancholy and sense of longing on that battleship that night?

As they enjoyed the show, the crew members had no idea of the surprise that the ship's chaplain, E.P. Wuebbens, had arranged. He had collected $5 from each sailor who had children at home. The total was $2,404.25. The chaplain then sent the money to Macy's department store, along with the names and addresses of the 729 children of the crew members. Chaplain Wuebbens asked Macy's to send a $3 gift to each child, with a card attached that said that the gift was from a loved one and his shipmates on the USS North Carolina. The chaplain wrote to Macy's, "We realize that we are asking a great deal, but . . . you will be adding greatly to the happiness of our children and to our own Christmas joy out here in one of the war zones. Incidentally we hope that a bit of that joy will reflect on you and your staff of workers."

Macy's filled the chaplain's request — and even more! Macy's invited the mothers and children who were able to travel to come to the store. They were filmed opening their presents and sending Christmas hellos and love to their fathers and husbands. When the Christmas Eve skits and comedy bits were finished on that battleship, the lights were dimmed and the movie was shown. In a story in *Our State* magazine about that special Christmas Eve in the South Pacific, Susan Stafford Kelly described "A longing too deep to describe, a homesickness too great to express, a surprise too joyous to ever forget."[3]

That is the Advent promise today as we think about going home for Christmas. In this time between the times, in this already-but-not yet between Christ's first Advent and his coming again, we experience "a longing too deep to describe, a homesickness too great to express." But we also rejoice at "a surprise too joyous to ever forget."

Courage! Take heart!

God is here, right here, on his way to put things right

and redress all wrongs.

He's on his way! He'll save you!

NOTES

[1]Susanna Spencer, "12 Secular Christmas Songs that are Actually About Advent," at www.churchpop.com.

[2]David Marine, "The Story of I'll Be Home for Christmas and the Battleship North Carolina," at www.blog.coldwellbanker.com.

[3]Susan Stafford Kelly, "Christmas Aboard the USS *North Carolina*," at www.ourstate.com.

Putting Joseph in the Manger Scene
Isaiah 7:10-17; Matthew 1:18-25

When my family decorated our Christmas tree and house when I was a kid, my job was to set up the manger scene. Each year I would carefully unwrap each figure and carefully place the figures just right in the cardboard stable. I don't know when my mom and dad bought the creche scene, but by the time I was given the job of setting it up, it was already looking kind of worn. The orangish-pink cow was missing an ear. The cardboard stable was sagging in several places and was stapled together. Still, I loved setting up that manger scene. I even drew a picture of the scene and wrote "Manger Scene and People" on the box it was packed in.

When my mom sold her house and downsized, she passed the manger scene on to me. For several years, when Nancy and I decorated for Christmas, I would pull out the "Manger Scene and People" box and carefully set up the figures. Finally, after a number of years, I sadly had to admit that it was time to retire my childhood manger scene.

In 1994, Nancy and I bought twelve pecan resin manger scene figurines to paint. The whole crew was present: Mary, Joseph, the baby Jesus, three wise men, two shepherds, a camel, a sheep, a cow, and a donkey. We had a good time deciding what colors to use for each character and what expressions to put on their faces. I still enjoy unwrapping the figures each year and arranging them in the living room fireplace. Last week, as we were decorating the house, I carefully unwrapped each figure. When I unwrapped Joseph, I realized (once again — I forget every year!) that Joseph is the only unfinished figure. His brown robe and green cloak are painted, but his feet, hands, face, and head covering are still the light tan color of the pecan resin. Also, poor Joseph has something of a blank stare, almost as if he is anonymous. I don't remember why Joseph didn't get finished. My hunch is it's because Natalie arrived in our family in August 1994, and with two children in the house, any spare time for painting figurines was suddenly gone!

Nancy and I weren't making any sort of theological statement by leaving Joseph unfinished. However, in early versions of creche scenes, Joseph is often left out or, if he happens to be present, he is in the background. In fact, in very many early manger scenes, Joseph is depicted as turned away from the baby Jesus and/or with a frown on his face — so much so that he is sometimes referred to as "grumpy Joseph."

In one particular religious icon of the Nativity, the focus is on the baby Jesus and his mother, Mary. Interestingly, Mary is not looking at her newborn son. Instead, she is turned away and looking at Joseph, who is seated in the lower left-hand corner. Joseph's head is bowed and he rests his cheek on his left hand. He is talking with Satan, who is disguised as an old shepherd. The suggestion is that Satan is trying to sow more doubts in Joseph's mind about what is taking place.

One description of this icon of the Nativity says, "The posture of St. Joseph is one of doubt and inner trouble, for he wondered if it might be possible that the conception and birth were not by some secret human union . . . Mary is shown larger than any of the other figures, reclining on a mat, and looking not at her new-born Son, but rather with love and compassion towards her spouse, St. Joseph the Betrothed, seeing his affliction and bewilderment over this most strange and divine birth."[1]

Far be it from me to criticize or correct iconic religious art, but that particular picture of Joseph seems out of order. If Joseph had any misgivings and questions about what was happening with Mary being pregnant, it was **before** Mary had borne a son. And, honestly, who can blame Joseph if he did have misgivings and questions about what was happening with Mary? My Bible translation says "Mary had been engaged to Joseph" when "she was found to be with child from the Holy Spirit." The King James Version reads, "was espoused to Joseph." That "engagement" was different from what we think of as an engagement. Mary and Joseph's "engagement" would have been arranged by their parents. Even though they each lived with their parents until they were married, they were pledged to one another legally. Mary's unexpected pregnancy was a crisis, to say the least.

What would the neighbors think? If a young, betrothed woman suddenly turns up pregnant, there are only two possibilities: either she had slept with the man to whom she was betrothed or she had slept with another man. Joseph knew the first wasn't true, which meant the second must be. So, Joseph was justified in seeking a divorce from Mary. In fact, Joseph would have been justified in seeking more than a divorce. He could have publicly shamed and humiliated Mary. He could have sought her death for her apparent adultery. Maybe there were some people in the village who thought that's exactly what Joseph should have done.

That's when Joseph was probably sitting on a rock with his head in his hands, talking with Satan who was planting seeds of doubt in Joseph's mind. But Matthew tells us something very important about Joseph, even though we don't know very much at all about Jesus' earthly father. Matthew 1:19 says, "Her husband Joseph, being a righteous man and unwilling to expose her to public disgrace, planned to dismiss her quietly."

At the Presbyterian Men's Christmas dinner at the Rose Hill Restaurant a couple of weeks ago, Rev. Bill Goodnight read Matthew's Christmas story and then made a profound statement. Bill said about Joseph, "He was a righteous man, but he was not a legalist." In other words, Joseph wanted to do the right thing in a difficult situation — the right thing for himself, the right thing for Mary, the right thing for God. On the one hand, Joseph's "righteousness" could have been measured by how faithful he was to the letter of the law when he found out Mary was pregnant. On the other hand, Joseph's "righteousness" was not defined by following the rules and toeing the line, but was tempered by mercy. So, Joseph planned to meet the minimum requirements of the law — he planned to dismiss Mary quietly.

Then Joseph had a dream, and the angel of the Lord said, "Joseph, son of David, do not be afraid to take Mary as your wife, for the child conceived in her is from the Holy Spirit." You would think that would take care of it — a word directly from the Lord through his angel messenger. Yet, Joseph is being asked to trust God's Word that seems to go against everything Joseph has been taught and believed. Joseph is being asked to trust God and to step out in faith on a journey that can't have been easy.

One preacher says this about Joseph (and us), "I might be able to muster the courage necessary to defy society's expectations in order to do the right thing. I might be able to act in faith to seek God's will, to look at scripture and to pray that God's will be done. I might have trust enough to believe that whatever situation God has presented me with will turn out well, and for the good, not just for myself, and maybe not even for myself at all, but for the common good. I wonder at Joseph's response, and I wonder if I could be like him. I wonder at Joseph's love — his love for Mary, his love for his adopted son, and his love for God. . . What scene could ever convey the Christmas story, and in particular, the faith of Joseph throughout the year? Imagine seeing the nativity as Joseph does, seeing through lenses of courage and faith and trust. That's how God calls us to see the world, and our daily lives, and the events that surround us and confound us and overwhelm us and awe us. We are to be Josephs in this world — people of courage and faith and trust and love. People who are willing to suspend disbelief about what God is doing in our very midst this day."[2]

There is a story about a children's Christmas pageant that encountered a crisis at the last minute. As the children were putting on their costumes in the Fellowship Hall, the assistant director ran out of the room in a panic, crying, "We have no Joseph! We have no Joseph!" Then she calmed down enough to explain that the little boy who was supposed to be Joseph had developed a bad case of nausea right before he left his house (sounds like he might have been trying to get out of being in the pageant!). Very calmly, the pageant director came up with a solution, "Well, let a shepherd stand a little closer to the manger with Mary. Nobody will notice Joseph's absence. He has no speaking part in the story."[3]

It's easy to overlook Joseph in the manger, even in the whole Christmas story. In Luke's Christmas story, Mary has all of the speaking parts, especially before the baby is born, when she sings praises to God and says, "Here I am, the servant of the Lord; let it be with me according to your word." (Luke 1:38)

A quick review of Christmas hymns in our *Glory to God* hymnal shows a distinct bias toward Mary:

* "To you this night is born a child of Mary, chosen and virgin mild"

* "For Christ is born of Mary . . ."

* "'round yon virgin mother and child!"

* "The virgin's tender arms enfolding, warm and safe the child are holding"

* "Isaiah 'twas foretold it, the rose I have in mind; with Mary we behold it, the virgin mother kind."

* "That boy-child of Mary was born in a stable, a manger his cradle in Bethlehem"

* "Once in royal David's city stood a lowly cattle shed, where a mother laid her baby in a manger for his bed: Mary was that mother mild; Jesus Christ, her little child"

* "Gentle Mary laid her child lowly in a manger"

It's true — Joseph doesn't say a word in Matthew's Christmas story. But what Joseph does, in faithful response to the Lord's message through his angel, speaks just as clearly and loudly as Mary saying, "Here I am, the servant of the Lord; let it be with me according to your word." Obviously, if we didn't have Mary and the baby Jesus in the manger scene, we wouldn't have much of a Christmas story. But let's not be so quick to say with that pageant director, "Nobody will notice Joseph's absence."

It's time we put Joseph in the manger scene — not just in our Christmas pageants and creche scene decorations, but in our lives as followers of Jesus Christ. Another preacher has put it this way: "[Joseph] was an ordinary man trying his best to listen to God. And his willingness to serve God turned out to be enough: he had a role to play in the larger drama of salvation. . . Joseph did not refuse to do 'the something' that he could do, and so Jesus the Messiah was born and life was changed forever. What helps you to listen deeply to the voice of love that is speaking within *you*? What is love calling *you* to do or say? With Joseph beside us to encourage us and give us strength, perhaps we too will respond and will follow where love leads. Perhaps we too will stand with Joseph in that Bethlehem stable, gazing at the newborn Jesus and marveling at the ways of God."[4]

Maybe it's time to get out the paintbrushes and paint and finish painting Joseph, so we can put a complete Joseph in the manger scene where he belongs.

NOTES

[1] "Explanation of the Nativity Icon," January 6, 2010, Church of the Nativity at www.churchofthenativity.net.

[2] Rev. Beth Neel, "Nativity," December 22, 2013 at www.westprespdx.org.

[3] Rev. Dr. Joanna Seibert, "Joseph's Part in the Christmas Pageant," December 22, 2o13 at St. Luke's Episcopal Church, North Little Rock, AK at www.stlukeespicopal.org.

[4] Rev. Margaret Bulitt-Jones, "Another look at Joseph," at St. John's Church, Ashfield, MA, December 22, 2013 at www.revivingcreation.org.

In Line with Sinners
Romans 6:1-11; Luke 3:1-22

On Saturday, November 21, 2015, a church in Harlem in New York City overflowed with sinners lined up for the chance to scrub their records clean. Anthony King, 28, said, "It's a pretty long line but it's a good idea." Another sinner in line, 25-year-old Letice Yates said, "It's time to clean up my act and change my life." Wouldn't that be something? To have people lined up outside the church doors, waiting to scrub their records clean, clean up their acts, and change their lives?

Actually, what happened in Harlem on that Saturday in November wasn't exactly as I have presented it. Here are the opening sentences of the newspaper article about the event: "A Harlem church overflowed with sinners Saturday as hundreds of petty criminals lined up for the chance to scrub their records clean. The one-day event was launched by the Manhattan District Attorney's office to give New Yorkers the opportunity to resolve warrants stemming from low-level crimes such as public urination, public drinking, and pot possession. As many as 200 scofflaws stood in a line that stretched down West 124th Street, outside Soul Saving Station Church, to gain their absolution." The article ended this way: "Some people were a little wary of the opportunity, thinking it might be a trap. There were no arrests made during the amnesty event, the first of its kind in Manhattan."[1]

Standing in line with sinners — That image stuck in my mind as I read today's gospel story about John the Baptist preaching a baptism of repentance for the forgiveness of sins. Can you see yourself standing in a line of sinners?

Last Sunday afternoon, a church in Leland, NC was full of sinners lined up for the chance to "receive the sustaining presence of Christ, remember God's covenant promise, and pledge their obedience anew."

Dr. Doug Cushing was installed as the first pastor of the bridge Presbyterian Church in Leland. Doug has served as the organizing pastor of this new church development for about three years. Sunday's installation service was the answer to many prayers and a time for great celebration.

During the worship service, we celebrated the Sacrament of the Lord's Supper. Doug instructed the gathered folks that we would take the bread and cup by coming forward, tearing a piece of bread and dipping it in the cup. He then invited us to come to our Lord's table: "Come forward and receive the bread and cup.'

This was a rare and welcome opportunity for me to be on that end of communion. That typically happens only at presbytery meetings or on pastor retreats. Whenever we receive the bread and cup by intinction, I like to watch all of the people going forward. I like being in the line, waiting my turn to tear the bread and dip it in the cup and hear the words, "The body and blood of Christ for you." As a sinner myself, it's a powerful experience to be in line with a bunch of sinners.

Imagine the scene there in the wilderness by the Jordan River. Imagine Jesus standing in line, waiting his turn to be baptized by John. What do you see? What do you think the people standing in line with Jesus saw when they looked at him?

Did you know that we have no physical description of Jesus in the gospels? The closest we come to any kind of description is when Mark in his gospel and Philip in the Book of Acts cite the Suffering Servant passage from the prophet Isaiah: "Just as there were many who were astonished at him — so marred was his appearance, beyond human semblance, and his form beyond that of mortals . . . He had no form or majesty that we should look at him, nothing in his appearance that we should desire him. He was despised and rejected by others; a man of suffering and acquainted with infirmity; and as one from whom others hide their faces he was despised, and we held him of no account." (Isaiah 52:14; 53:2-3)

But what did Jesus look like? Well, he probably looked like any other 1st century A.D. Palestinian Jew. Look at the picture in the upper left hand corner on the front page of today's bulletin.

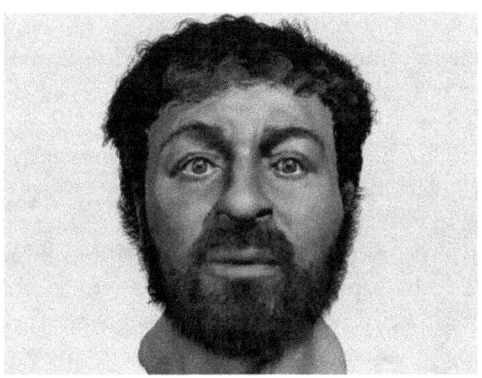

Is that what Jesus looked like? Who knows? That picture was generated by Richard Neave, a retired medical artist from the University of Manchester, England, in 2001 for a BBC documentary. Mr. Neave used an actual skull of a 1st century Palestinian man. He said, "I made a plaster cast of the skull which gives me something to work on. Then I put clay over it and, using soft tissue measurements, build up the anatomy of the face. Inevitably there are some areas where you have to speculate, particularly if parts of the skull are missing." Mr. Neave did not make the claim that this is actually Jesus' face, but that, if Jesus looked like a man of his time and place in 1st century A.D. Palestine, he might have/probably looked like this.[2]

It's different, isn't it? The point is, unless you were a neighbor of Jesus from Nazareth standing in line with him by the Jordan River, you probably wouldn't have noticed anything different about him. At this point in the gospel, Jesus has yet to begin his public ministry of preaching, healing, and teaching. The general public wouldn't have known about him. He was/is one of us. As *The Message* translates John 1:14, "The Word became flesh and blood, and moved into the neighborhood."

Wait a minute! Even if Jesus looked like a man of his time and place, which meant he looked like everybody else in line for baptism that day, wasn't he different? John "went into all the region around the Jordan, proclaiming a baptism of repentance for the forgiveness of sins." (Luke 3:3) Why did Jesus have to be baptized? After all, as Hebrews 4:14-15 reminds us, "Since, then, we have a great high priest who has passed through the heavens, Jesus, the Son of God, let us hold fast to our confession. For we do not have a high priest who is unable to sympathize with our weaknesses, but we have one who in every respect has been tested as we are, yet without sin."

Why did Jesus have to be baptized? It depends on what you mean by "have to." Already in the time when the gospels were being written, this was an embarrassing question for the church. In Matthew's story, when Jesus goes to be baptized by John, John protests and says, "I need to be baptized by you, and do you come to me?" But Jesus tells him, "Let it be so now; for it is proper for us in this way to fulfill all righteousness." (Matthew 3:14-15)

In other words, it was "necessary, the right thing to do," just as the boy Jesus "had to" be in the temple, being about his Father's business. This is what Jesus chose to do. He submitted to God's will and stood in solidarity with us. As someone has said, "Jesus comes to join and not abandon the people of God. Jesus wasn't ashamed, he was there with everybody to be baptized. Jesus simply got in line with everybody who had been broken by the wear and tear of the world." Which is why the letter to the Hebrews can go on to say, "Let us therefore approach the throne of grace with boldness, so that we may receive mercy and find grace to help in time of need." (4:16)

That's why it is such good news that Jesus stood in line with sinners that day by the Jordan, waiting to get baptized. That's why it is such good news that Jesus still stands with sinners like you and me today.

In the last couple of weeks, we have heard from Luke's gospel that "the child grew and became strong, filled with wisdom; and the favor of God was upon him . . .and Jesus increased in wisdom and in years, and in divine and human favor." When Jesus had been baptized, a heavenly voice told him, "You are my Son, the Beloved; with you I am well pleased." Maybe God the Father was well pleased that Jesus had gone to the water to be baptized. But God was probably most pleased about the arc of Jesus' life and what it suggested about his upcoming ministry.

Jesus standing in line with sinners is a preview of what is to come. That is the complaint lodged against him throughout the gospel of Luke:

> * When Jesus and his disciples went to dinner at the house of Levi the tax collector, along with a large crowd of tax collectors, the Pharisees and their scribes complained to the disciples, "Why do you eat and drink with tax collectors?" (Luke 5:29-30)
>
> * When a woman from the city barged in and bathed Jesus' feet at the dinner party at the Simon the Pharisee's house, the host thought to himself, "If this man were a prophet, he would have known who and what kind of woman this is who is touching him — that she is a sinner." (Luke 7:39)
>
> * When all the tax collectors and sinners came to listen to Jesus, the Pharisees and scribes grumbled, "This fellow welcomes sinners and eats with them." (Luke 15:2)
>
> * When Jesus invited himself to dinner at the home of the tax collector Zacchaeus, everybody grumbled, "He has gone to be the guest of one who is a sinner." (Luke 19:6-7)

Do you wonder what Jesus thought about as he stood in line with sinners and looked at all of them? Jesus once told his disciples a parable about a Pharisee and a tax collector praying in the temple. The Pharisee prayed, "God, I thank you that I am not like other people; thieves, rogues, adulterers, or even like this tax collector." (Luke 18:11) If anyone in history could have ever prayed that Pharisee's prayer in all truth and sincerity, it was Jesus. But, not only did Jesus never pray that way, his life, ministry, and death showed just the opposite reaction to the people in line with him:

> * he came to be baptized with all the people

> * he came as an act of solidarity with a nation and world of sinners
>
> * he got in line with a bunch of sin-sick people who were looking for a new beginning and a return to God
>
> * he identified with the broken sinners who needed God.

The beautiful Christ hymn in Philippians 2 puts it this way: "Let the same mind be in you that was in Christ Jesus, who, though he was in the form of God, did not regard equality with God as something to be exploited, but emptied himself, taking the form of a slave, being born in human likeness. And being found in human form, he humbled himself and became obedient to the point of death — even death on a cross." (2:5-8)

Even though our own baptisms and those of our children are occasions for great celebration as we are reminded, "You are children of God," baptism reminds us of the great cost of God's love in the life and death of his Beloved Son. In his letter to the Christians at Rome, just before the section Ann read this morning about dying and rising with Christ in baptism, the apostle Paul writes, "For while we were still weak, at the right time Christ died for the ungodly. Indeed, rarely will anyone die for a righteous person — though perhaps for a good person someone might actually dare to die. But God proves his love for us in that while we still were sinners Christ died for us. Much more surely then, now that we have been justified by his blood, will we be saved through him from the wrath of God. For if while we were enemies, we were reconciled to God through the death of his Son, much more surely, having been reconciled, will we be saved by his life." (Romans 5:6-10)

Aren't you glad that Jesus got in line with sinners like you and me that day by the Jordan River?

NOTES

[1]Melkorka Licea, "Sinners line up outside church to resolve low-level crimes," November 21, 2015, www.nypost.com.

[2]Michael Morrow, "Experts use forensics tests to discover what Jesus Christ may have look like," December 16, 2015, www.news.com.au.

Journey to the Cross

The Jesus Paradox
Colossians 1:15-20; Mark 9:9-13, 30-37

A man stumbled in through the front door of his house after a long day at work. His face was red, he was out of breath, his clothes were dirty, and he was sweating heavily. His wife looked at him and said, "My goodness! What in the world happened to you?" The man said, "I just ran all the way home behind a bus, and I saved $1." His wife shook her head and said, "You fool! You could have run home behind a taxi cab and saved $10!"

That story sounds a lot like what happened to me a week ago when I went to Belk in Wilmington to buy a new suit. After the clerk had rung up the sale, I had swiped my credit card and signed the receipt, and he had put the suit in a bag, he handed me the suit bag and said, "Thank you, Mr. Gladden. You saved $330 today." As I walked away, I thought to myself, "If I hadn't spent any money, I would have saved $550!" (Of course, I also wouldn't have a new suit, which I really need!)

I guess my experience in Belk proves the old saying, "You can save money by spending it." That statement is a classic paradox, which Webster's New World Dictionary defines as "a statement that seems contradictory, unbelievable, or absurd but that may actually be true."

There is an ancient Chinese folk tale from the 3rd century B.C. about a blacksmith who was trying to sell a spear and a shield he had made. A potential customer asked him how good his spear was. He replied that it could pierce any shield. When the customer asked him how good his shield was, he said it could defend you against all spear attacks. The customer thought for a minute, then asked the blacksmith what would happen if he struck his shield with his spear. The blacksmith had no answer. As a result, the Chinese word for "self-contradictory" or "paradox" is made up of two characters, one for spear, one for shield.[1]

Here are some paradoxical statements:

* Oscar Wilde wrote, "I can resist anything except temptation."

* Socrates wrote: "I know one thing, that I know nothing."

* "Deep down, you're really shallow."

* "Nobody goes to that restaurant anymore because it's too crowded."

* Yogi Berra said, "Baseball is 90% mental and the other half is physical" and, talking about the problems with the sun in left field at Yankee Stadium, "It gets late early out here."

What about these paradoxical statements?

* "The Son of Man is to be betrayed into human hands, and they will kill him, and three days after being killed, he will rise again." (Mark 9:31)

* "Whoever wants to be first must be last of all and servant of all." (Mark 9:35)

* "For those who want to save their life will lose it, and those who lose their life for my sake, and for the sake of the gospel, will save it." (Mark 8:35)

* "God has made him both Lord and Messiah, this Jesus whom you crucified." (Acts 2:36)

Jesus as the crucified Lord of glory is a paradox. He was 2000 years ago. He still is today. The description of "paradox" and its literary use talks about "a person having seemingly contradictory qualities." A rhetorical paradox is when a character makes a seemingly inconsistent or contradictory statement, such as when Jesus talks about the Son of Man being handed over to suffer and die on a cross. A situational paradox is when characters find themselves in difficult to reconcile circumstances, such as when Peter makes the true confession of faith, "You are the Messiah," only to be told by Jesus that he must suffer and die in Jerusalem.[2]

Three times in this middle section of Mark's gospel, Jesus tells his disciples that he is on his way to Jerusalem to suffer and die and rise again. Each time the disciples learn a little bit more about who Jesus is, Jesus talks about suffering and dying. The disciples misunderstand and Jesus has to correct them.

* When Jesus asked, "Who do you say that I am?" Peter correctly answered, "You are the Messiah." Then Jesus told all of his disciples he was going to suffer and die. Peter rebuked him. Jesus rebuked Peter, and talked about what it means to be his disciple and follow him ("take up your cross").

* When Peter, James, and John were coming down the mountain with Jesus after they got a glimpse of his resurrection glory in the Transfiguration, Jesus talked with them about going to Jerusalem to suffer and die. A little bit later, the disciples argued among themselves about who is the greatest. Jesus taught them about what it means to be his follower ("the first must be last").

* When the disciples were following Jesus on the road to Jerusalem, amazed at everything they had seen and heard, Jesus told them what was going to happen to him when they got to Jerusalem. James and John asked Jesus for positions of power and authority in his coming kingdom, and Jesus taught them all what it means to be his follower ("whoever wishes to be great must be a servant; whoever wishes to be first must be slave of all; the Son of Man came not to be served but to serve, and to give his life as a ransom for many").

That's all very interesting, but what's it got to do with us? Someone asked the other day, "What if the disciples *had* asked Jesus to explain what they didn't understand?" Well, actually, he does just that, by telling them three times on the way to Jerusalem what is going to happen to him and why. Mark is quite up-front in telling us, "But they did not understand what he was saying and were afraid to ask him." (Mark 9:32)

But why? When I was in seminary, there were several times when I didn't understand what a professor was talking about in his or her lecture. Far too many times I didn't ask because I didn't want to look stupid or I didn't think I knew enough to ask about what I didn't know (there's a paradox for you!) or I was just plain intimidated by the professor (my problem, not theirs!). Maybe that's why the disciples were afraid to ask Jesus about what they didn't understand.

Or, maybe they were afraid to ask because they really didn't want to hear what he might say. After all, Jesus had already talked to them twice about going up to Jerusalem in order to suffer and die, and then he had told them what it meant for them to be his followers: "Deny yourselves, take up your cross daily, and follow me."

Maybe that's why we "don't ask" and do our best to avoid the cross. I read a comment this week about how people crowd churches for Easter Sunday services, but not for Good Friday services, "We are always tempted to make a detour around the Cross in favor of the open tomb." In his 1937 book *The Cost of Discipleship,* Dietrich Bonhoeffer used the term "cheap grace" to describe our tendency and desire to avoid the demands and costs of following Jesus. He described "cheap grace" as "the preaching of forgiveness without requiring repentance, baptism without church discipline. Communion without confession. Cheap grace is grace without discipleship, grace without the cross, grace without Jesus Christ, living and incarnate."[3]

We are always tempted to make a detour around the Cross in favor of the open tomb because the Jesus paradox is hard for us to grasp, even today. A crucified Messiah, a Savior nailed to a cross — these are supreme paradoxes. Yet, we live in a world in which certain, contrary ideas seem to hold true, at least from the world's perspective:

* Might makes right.

* Only the strong survive.

* The Golden Rule: He who has the gold makes the rules.

* Winning isn't everything; it's the only thing.

No wonder, then, that the apostle Paul says that the message about the cross is foolishness and a stumbling block. It was then, it is now.

Philip Gladden

My beloved professor and mentor, Dr. Paul Achtemeier ("Bud") wrote about two "mind-bending paradoxes" of Jesus' life, death and resurrection:

> * The Son of the God who created the world and humankind is put to death by the very creatures God created.

> * The only way life can find greatness is through the renunciation of the search for greatness.[4]

On this Lenten journey to the cross, we are reading stories about Jesus and his disciples on the way, on the road, on a journey to Jerusalem. This is more than a geographical itinerary; it is a theological map that leads to the reality that the Son of Man must be handed over and killed. But, remember a definition of a paradox? "A statement that seems contradictory, unbelievable, or absurd but that may actually be true." The crucified Lord of glory — the Lord and Messiah, this Jesus whom you crucified — in him, this paradoxical Jesus, we have our hope.

Near the end of Mark's gospel, as Jesus hangs dying on the cross, the passersby deride him and say, "Save yourself, and come down from the cross!" In the same way the chief priests, along with the scribes, were also mocking him among themselves and saying, "He saved others; he cannot save himself." (Mark 15:29-31) I don't know if those statements qualify as paradoxes, but they are certainly full of irony. The passersby and the religious officials were mocking, but they spoke the truth: By not saving himself, Jesus saved others. That's the point.

Geoffrey R. King puts into words the ultimate paradox of our Christian faith when he says, "Here is a faith which offers to the world life . . . and the badge of it is the symbol of death." The cross has been called "the sign of contradiction." We do proclaim a paradoxical faith: "The Word became flesh and lived among us, and we have seen his glory, the glory as of a father's only son." (John 1:14) "May I never boast of anything except the cross of our Lord Jesus Christ, by which the world has been crucified to me, and I to the world."

(Galatians 6:14) "The message about the cross is the power of God and the wisdom of God." (1 Corinthians 1:18, 24)

The great bishop of North Africa in the 4th century A.D., St. Augustine, describes the Jesus paradox this way: "The deformity of Christ forms you. If he had not willed to be deformed, you would not have recovered the form which you had lost. Therefore he was deformed when he hung on the cross. But his deformity is our comeliness. In this life, therefore, let us hold fast to the deformed Christ." (from his *Discourses on the Psalms*)

Thanks be to God that we have and serve a Lord and Savior and Messiah who was crucified for our sakes, but who has been raised from the dead that we might live for God always.

NOTES

[1] Charles Moffat, "The Unstoppable Force Vs Immovable Object Paradox," www.nerdovore.com.

[2] "Paradox," at www.literarydevices.com.

[3] Dietrich Bonhoeffer, *The Cost of Discipleship* (New York: MacMillan Publishing Co., Inc., 1937), p. 47.

[4] Paul J. Achtemeier, "Mark 9:30-37," *Interpretation*, April 1976, p. 183.

Journey to the Cross

May I Have This Dance?
Romans 12:1-2, 9-21; Mark 10:32-45

The deejay at our niece's wedding reception was one of the best we've ever heard. He played continuously for four hours, never taking a break. After we finished eating dinner, Nancy and I went out on the dance floor. As the evening wore on, we noticed we were dancing in the midst of a bunch of 20-something young adults. Then we realized our dance moves didn't really fit with the music the deejay was playing. Then we realized we really didn't know the songs the deejay was playing. Then we realized we were out of step, out of sync on the dance floor, in more ways than one. Then we went back to our table and sat down and watched. Oh well, it was fun while it lasted!

In his commentary on the gospel of Mark, Lamar Williamson describes the disciples' lack of understanding when Jesus repeatedly talks about going to Jerusalem to suffer and die. He writes, "The disciples have heard Jesus' words, but they have the music all wrong. They still dance to the world's tune."[1]

This morning, as you hear another story from Mark's gospel about Jesus telling his disciples he must go to Jerusalem to die and their misunderstanding, confusion, and inappropriate response, think about Jesus asking, "May I have this dance?" Notice the margin note in today's bulletin next to the Opening Sentences: "When Jesus died for you he was, as it were, inviting you into the dance. He invites you to begin centering everything in your life on him, even as he has given himself for you."[2]

Will we, like the disciples, continue to dance to the world's tune? Or will we dance with Jesus? Either way we will be out of step, out of sync, either with the world or with Jesus. Which will it be?

We may be much more comfortable dancing to the world's tune, because we already know the steps and moves so well. But dancing that way leads to:

* Peter rebuking Jesus when he talked about going to Jerusalem to die (Mark 8:33). Jesus had to rebuke Peter, "Get behind me, Satan! for you are setting your mind not on divine things but on human things."

* The disciples arguing among themselves about who was the greatest (9:34). They must have been ashamed, for when Jesus asked them, "What were you arguing about on the way?" . . . "they were silent, for on the way they had argued with one another who was the greatest."

* James and John asking for positions of authority on Jesus' right and left hands in his earthly kingdom (Mark 10:42-43). Jesus had to remind all of the disciples that the Gentile rulers lorded it over their subjects and their "great ones" were tyrants.

In other words, when we dance to the world's tune, we become self-centered and self-seeking. Instead of accepting Jesus' invitation, we try to make him dance to our own tune. Isn't that what the devil tried to do when he tempted Jesus to be something other than the Messiah he was meant to be? Isn't that what Peter tried to do when he scolded Jesus and, we can assume, said something like, "Messiahs don't suffer and die"? As one writer has put it, "Even worse, the disciples sometimes put themselves at cross purposes with Jesus by trying to educate their teacher about proper messianic behavior."[3]

But there's another tune to dance to, and the refrain goes like this: "The Son of Man must undergo great suffering, and be handed over to the chief priests and the scribes, and they will condemn him to death; and after three days he will rise again." Do we recognize the song? Does it make us want to dance with Jesus? If so, we'll have to learn a whole new set of dance steps and moves. It may be awkward and difficult, because dancing to this tune means:

* Deny yourselves, take up your cross, and follow me (Mark 8:34).

> * Whoever wants to be first must be last of all and servant of all (Mark 9:35).
>
> * Whoever wishes to become great among you must be your servant, and whoever wishes to be first among you must be slave of all (Mark 10:43-44).

We don't often think about Jesus dancing. But what if he did? And what if he invited his followers to join him?

In the second century A.D., numerous tales were written about the adventures of Jesus' disciples. One is called *The Acts of John*, which contains stories about the missionary activities of John, the son of Zebedee (who appears in today's gospel story). Near the end of the "book," John describes what happened on the night before Jesus was arrested and crucified. We know from Matthew, Mark, Luke, and John that Jesus ate the Passover meal and washed his disciples' feet. In *The Acts of John*, John says, "Now, before he was arrested . . . he gathered us all together and said, 'Before I am delivered up to them, let us sing a hymn to the Father, and go forth to what lies before us.' So he commanded us to make a circle, holding one another's hands, and he himself stood in the middle. He said, 'Respond Amen to me.' He then began to sing a hymn, and to say, 'Glory be to you, Father!' And we circling him said, 'Amen.' 'Glory be to you, Word! Glory be to you, Grace!' 'Amen.' 'Glory be to you, Spirit! Glory be to you, Holy One! Glory be to the glory!' 'Amen.' 'We praise you, O Father. We give thanks to you, light, in whom darkness does not abide.' 'Amen.'"

The song and the dancing continue, " 'I will pipe, dance all of you!' 'Amen.' 'The whole universe is dancing above.' 'Amen.' 'He who does not dance, does not know what is being done.' 'Amen.' 'Now if you respond to my dancing, see yourself in me who speak . . .You who dance, perceive what I do.'" John then says, "After this dance, my beloved the Lord went out. . . Even I, when I saw him suffer, did not abide at his passion but fled to the Mount of Olives, weeping over what had taken place. And . . . he was hung upon the cross on Friday, at the sixth hour of the day."[4]

Scholars think this story might be the basis for an ancient Christian liturgical dance. Dance is often used to describe the dynamic and intimate relationship between God and his people, and even among the Father, Son, and Holy Spirit. The "dance of God" or the "dance of the Holy Trinity" is called *perichoresis*, which means "rotation" or "a going around." You can hear the word "choreography" in there. Timothy Keller describes that intimate and intertwined relationship of the Trinity this way: "When we delight and serve someone else, we enter into a dynamic orbit around him or her, we center on the interests and desires of the other. That creates a dance, particularly if there are three persons, each of whom moves around the other two . . . None demands that the others revolve around him. Each voluntarily circles the other two, pouring love, delight, and adoration into them . . . That creates a dynamic, pulsating dance of joy and love."[5]

"Dance, then, wherever you may be; I am the Lord of the Dance, said, he, and I'll lead you all, wherever you may be, and I'll lead you all in the dance, said he." (Refrain, Hymn #157, "I Danced in the Morning," *Glory to God*)

According to the Arthur Murray Dance Centers website, when you dance, you have The Leader and The Follower. The Leader "communicates the patterns of a dance through decisive movement." The Follower "is sensitive to the signals of a leader and responds accordingly."

Jesus, the Leader of the dance, sets the patterns of his dance: servanthood, cross-bearing, discipleship, the first must be last, the greatest must be the servant of all.

Jesus, the Leader of the dance, sets the patterns of his dance through decisive movement: on the road to Jerusalem, it is necessary for him to be handed over to die, "the Son of Man came not to be served but to serve, and to give his life as a ransom for many."

If Jesus is the Leader of the dance, that makes us the Follower. Who will we dance with? Will we follow the Leader or will we continue to dance to the world's tune? According to the Arthur Murray instructions, "Leader or follower, whichever role you choose to occupy is, quite literally, your job description on the dance floor. What you do with that responsibility will determine who you can dance with." Jesus has chosen his job description as the Leader of the dance. He says, "Follow me. Dance like this." Our job description in the Divine Dance is to be the followers. The steps are laid out for us, but they're hard to learn. We step all over Jesus' and our own feet. We stumble along. When I was looking for quotes for this week's bulletin margin notes, I Google searched "Jesus, discipleship, cross, follow me." I found a website called BoardofWisdom.com that had this saying of Jesus: "Whoever wants to be great among you must be your servant." Underneath this quote I saw this note: "This quote by Jesus of Nazareth is a favorite of 0 users." In other words, lots of time, we'd rather sit out the dance.

But Jesus is a persistent and winsome dance partner. He continues to hold out his nail-scarred hands and invite us into his divine dance of life. In 1883, William B. Sandy published his *Christmas Carols Ancient and Modern*. The collection contained a "traditional" English carol called "Tomorrow Shall Be My Dancing Day." The eleven-verse carol tells the story of Jesus' life, death, and resurrection as a dance, with the chorus, "Sing, oh! my love, oh! my love, my love, my love, This have I done for my true love." His birth and baptism are "to call my true love to my dance." His temptation was "to have me break my true love's dance." The religious and political leaders "judged me to die to lead the dance." He died on the cross "to call my true love to my dance." He rose again on the third day "up to my true love and the dance." He ascended up to heaven where he sits on the right hand of God, "that man may come unto the general dance."[6]

They say that you should always "dance with the one who brung ya." In other words, you should give proper fidelity and faithfulness to those who have gone out of their way to look after you. In 1993, Shania Twain released a popular song called "Dance with the One That Brought You." The chorus says, "You got to dance with the one that brought you, Stay with the one that wants you, The one who's gonna love you when all of the others go home. Don't let the green grass fool you, Don't let the moon get to you. Dance with the one that brought you and you can't go wrong."[7]

Jesus is the one who wants you. Jesus is the one who's gonna love you when all of the others go home. What will you say when Jesus holds out his hand, says "Follow me," and asks, "May I have this dance?"

Dance with Jesus, and you can't go wrong.

NOTES

[1] Lamar Williamson, Jr., *Mark* (Atlanta: John Knox Press, 1983), p. 193.

[2] Timothy Keller, *The Reason for God: Belief in an Age of Skepticism* (New York: Riverhead Books, 2008), p. 230.

[3] David Schnasa Jacobsen, "Between Text and Sermon, Mark 10:1-52," *Interpretation* April 2016, Vol. 70, No. 2, p. 194.

[4] Bart D. Ehrman, *Lost Scriptures: Books that Did Not Make It into the New Testament* (New York: Oxford University Press, 2003), pp. 105-106.

[5] Timothy Keller, *The Reason for God*, p. 224.

[6] "Tomorrow Shall Be My Dancing Day," at www.hymnsandcarolsofchristmas.com.

[7] Shania Twain, "Dance with the One That Brought You" at GooglePlayMusic at www.play.google.com.